BUILDING and EQUIPPING for CHRISTIAN EDUCATION

by C. HARRY ATKINSON

Published for the DEPARTMENT OF CHURCH BUILDING AND ARCHITECTURE
and the DEPARTMENT OF ADMINISTRATION AND LEADERSHIP

of the NATIONAL COUNCIL OF THE CHURCHES OF CHRIST IN THE U.S.A.

by the OFFICE OF PUBLICATION AND DISTRIBUTION

475 Riverside Drive, New York 27, New York

Library of Congress Catalog Card Number: 56—12731

PRICE $3.50

BB 06—827

Foreword..

"His vision foresaw the need
His genius created the design
His zeal consummated the plan."

These words are dedicated to an architect, Howard Van Doren Shaw, and inscribed on the fountain plaque in the lovely civic center in Lake Forrest, Illinois.

They are appropriate as a foreword to *Building and Equipping for Christian Education*. This much needed volume is the outgrowth of the Chicago Conference on Christian Education and Church Building, which met from September 30 through October 2, 1954. It is published for the Bureau of Church Building and the Department of Administration and Leadership of the National Council of Churches.

This conference was called by the Bureau of Church Building in co-operation with the Commission on General Christian Education—both bodies being agencies of the National Council of the Churches of Christ in the U.S.A., the Church Architectural Guild of America and, incidentally, the American Institute of Architecture. (See Note page 4.)

At the opening plenary session, C. Harry Atkinson, then Executive Director of the Bureau of Church Building, raised important points as helping to determine the success of the conference, for example:

The basic issues were: The critical importance of the Christian Education program; the fact that fifty cents of each building dolalr goes to the Christian Education building; plans already being decided revealed that there has been too much bad planning and poor management of space; noisy, poorly lighted, inadequately heated and ventilated teaching areas, with cold floors and damp atmosphere still characterize too many buildings; building criteria and forecasting are needed to keep pace with the rapid increase of population.

It was pointed out that guidance is needed at these specific points: grouping, projection and actual use of space, size and shape of teaching area; worship facilities; basic equipment according to age groups; audio-visual requirements; the gym-stage-fellowship-craft areas; the appraisal by the church of the community to determine the initial unit; and what the church-home pattern of many denominational curriculums implies about building needs.

The Christian education delegates were selected from denominational leaders who constitute such regular committees of the National Council of Churches as the Committees on: Children's Work (C.C.W.), Youth Work (C.Y.W.), Adult Work (C.A.W.), and Administration and Leadership (C.A.L.).

The National Council of Churches staff leaders in Audio-Visuals, Children's Work, Weekday Religious Education, Public Education, Curriculum, Research, Editorial, as well as executives from city and state Councils of Churches and Directors or Ministers of Christian Education from local churches participated.

Church architects who are also members of the American Institute of Architecture (A.I.A.) were selected by the Church Architectural Guild of America.

The national staffs of the Boards of Christian Education and Missions or Church Extension from fifteen major denominations* represented approximately 96,000 churches, with memberships totaling nearly 24,000,000. Thus 68 per cent of the churches and 66 per cent of the church membership of the National Council of Churches were represented in this conference.

The Chicago Conference was selective, bringing together the qualified persons. It was constituted by delegates chosen from the fields of Christian Education, Church Architecture and Church Building. They were divided into four working groups: preschool, elementary, youth and adult. The chairman of each group guided the discussion, and a recorder kept careful notes of the discussion held and the conclusions reached.

One of the most important things that happened at this conference, as far as Christian educators are concerned, was to show a united front when architects and builders may have felt there was a division among them. There were Lutherans and Presbyterians, Baptists and Methodists, meeting in various groups as recognized and responsible educators who had a common understanding and outlook. They spoke of the principles of Christian education in terms of program, and the architects and church builders were able to translate them into terms of building needs.

Very briefly, an evaluation might be something like this:

First, the Christian educators realized that the best architects, represented by those who were in attendance, had a real sympathy for the important edu-

---

* American Baptist Association; Church of the Brethren; Church of God (Anderson, Ind.); Church of the Nazarene; Congregational Christian Churches; Disciples of Christ International Convention; Evangelical and Reformed Church; Evangelical United Brethren Church; United Lutheran Church in America; Augustana Evangelical Lutheran; The Methodist Church; Presbyterian Church in the U.S.; Presbyterian Church in the U.S.A.; United Presbyterian Church of North America; United Church of Canada.

cational needs as they relate to church building. The interchange of ideas between the Christian educators and the architects and church builders proved that they spoke the same language.

Secondly, the Christian educators came to a better understanding of the problems architects face as they attempt to fit space for a particular age group into an over-all building plan. For example, the educators knew that the skeletal supporting structure of a building must be uniform on all floor levels, but had not realized the need to plan space for each age group in relation to the space for other age groups within the same building.

Thirdly, the Christian educators were able to clear up some educational principles with the architects. There was a mutual appreciation and agreement between the architects and the educators on the basic principles of building for Christian education.

Fourthly, Christian educators have a new appreciation of some of the problems that the architects face in their need to advise building committees on such items as furniture and equipment, floor covering, interior decoration, and the like. Perhaps the educators had not realized that the architect was responsible not only to design a plan that would be noble and inspiring, but also to give practical direction for furnishing the building.

Fifthly, the Christian educators had a very clear understanding of the relation of the building to the program. To be sure, Christian educators have long been speaking about building in terms of the total program. They were, however, pleased to find that the architects were at one with them in making this initial impact. This over-all view is of paramount significance in the development of a building plan.

Another result of this Conference is the replacement of Conover's *The Church School and Parish House Building* by this book written by Mr. Atkinson, in the light of authoritative, reflective thinking at the Chicago Conference.

We hope and believe that Christian educators and architects alike sense the importance of "vision" in relation to "need," of "genius" in relation to "design," and have "zeal" so that the "consummation" of our "plans" and our hopes for the future will be realized.

———

In 1941 the author of this book, C. Harry Atkinson, became Director of the Department of Edifice Funds and Building Counsel for the American Baptist Home Mission Society. In 1952, after eleven years of service in this capacity, he succeeded the late Elbert M. Conover, the first Executive Director of the Bureau of Church Building of the National Council of Churches. Four years later he became Editor of *Protestant Church Administration and Equipment* magazine.

At the 1956 annual meeting of the Church Architectural Guild of America, Mr. Atkinson received the coveted Elbert M. Conover architectural award in recognition of his contribution to better church architecture in this country.

Mr. Atkinson has been counseling churches and writing on church buildings for over fifteen years. He has visited upward of 3,000 church buildings and corresponded with some 10,000 churches in practically every state in the Union.

It should be understood that Mr. Atkinson has used all factual information and expert judgment which came out of each of the work groups of the Chicago Conference in this book. Whereas he recognized the need to state very briefly some basic points of the program and philosophy of Christian education, he would be the first to recommend that denominations turn to their own national sources for such guidance in this extremely important area. Finally, we owe a great deal to Mr. Atkinson, because he drew from his broad reading and experience in the field of counseling with churches and building committees; thus the color and flavor of his writing comes from the richness of his background.

SCOTT TURNER RITENOUR, *Chairman*
Conference on Christian Education
and Church Building

NOTE: Anthony Ferrara, A.I.A., Washington, D.C.; T. Norman Mansell, A.I.A., Philadelphia, Pa.; Benjamin Franklin Olson, A.I.A., Chicago, Ill.; Maurice R. Salo, A.I.A., New York, N. Y.; Donald Powers Smith, A.I.A., San Francisco, Calif.; Henry Steinbomer, A.I.A, San Antonio, Tex.; Walter A. Taylor, F.A.I.A., Washington, D.C.; Harold E. Wagoner, A.I.A., Philadelphia, Pa.; Arland A. Dirlam, A.I.A., Boston, Mass.; Robert L. Durham, F.A.I.A., Seattle, Wash.; Daniel D. Merrill, A.I.A., New York, N. Y.; Walk C. Jones, Jr., F.A.I.A., Memphis, Tenn.; Herbert J. Powell, F.A.I.A., San Marino, Calif.

A.I.A. indicates membership in the American Institute of Architects; F.A.I.A. indicates Fellow as well as member of A.I.A.

Table of Contents

CHAPTER 1

Today.....

New Eyes for Old Tasks

It was G. K. Chesterton who expressed the desire to enter his home after the fashion of a second-story burglar. He wanted to view it from a different vantage point so its deep satisfactions of love, shelter, and security might come to him with a fresh new joy. He wanted to make certain that the routine front door approach did not dull his eyes to the delights of a familiar scene.

In approaching its teaching ministry, the Christian Church might well emulate such a point of view. All too frequently the magnitude and the importance of this undertaking is lost sight of in the day by day routine of church life. What should be her major concern and her greatest joy settles into a listless, ineffective procedure carried on in drab surroundings by persons who lack training, enthusiasm, and a wholesome vision of the task in hand.

In these days when our scientific laboratories are unlocking world-shaking increments of energy, and secular concerns loom so large in the popular mind, we like to recall an incident which helps us to view the educational program of the church in a new light. It happened this way: A university student preparing for the Christian ministry showed an outstanding aptitude for scientific research. His professor urged him to abandon his chosen vocation of sharing the bread and wine at the altar of his church and to take in hand the test tube and retort of the laboratory. After some serious consideration, this insight flashed upon the mind of the student: The church is a spiritual laboratory. In this laboratory, we deal with human nature, "the subtlest, the most powerful and, in some respects, the most dangerous bundle of forces on the planet."[1]

The forces and factors to be shaped are the thoughts, the attitudes, and the lives of the persons who shape the world in which we live. We are endeavoring to bring the undisciplined possibilities of human personalities into vital contact with the transforming influence of the person of Jesus Christ. Skillfully consummated, the end result is new persons through whom the mind of Christ is made effective in all walks of life. The spiritual birth, growth, and integration of such persons into a fellowship of kindred minds dedicated to carrying out the will of God in all of life, together constitute the high mission of the Christian Church. The teacher who patiently deals with children, companions restless youth, and enriches the inner life of adults with such a vision will bring greater dedication to a creative and redemptive vocation.

In this connection we remember the words of William Temple: "We never know who is doing the greatest work for God. Here is a man who holds great office in the church and preaches to multitudes; yet at the end all he has done is to keep things from falling back. And there is a girl, poor and uneducated, of whom no one ever thinks; but because she, loving and devout, sows the seed in the life of a child entrusted to her care who grows to be a missionary pioneer or a Christian statesman, or a profound theologian, shapes the history of nations or the thought of generations."[2]

New Days Bring New Demands

The millions of children and youth now overcrowding our public school buildings present the church with an opportunity unparalleled in this country. Children numbering 31,292,000 were born in this country during the decade 1940-1950. There were 18,151,000 children under ten years of age in this country on May 1, 1955. Predictions indicate that this birth rate will be exceeded during the subsequent ten-year period.

The Christian nurture of the young parents of these millions of children adds a further responsibility in Christian education. Thanks to medical science and other factors, our elder citizens are living from twenty to twenty-five years longer than in 1900. This means fifty years of adult Christian education. Some 400,000 persons of sixty-five years of age and older are now being added yearly to our population. The Christian Church has never faced anything of such magnitude, so filled with promise, and so challenging.

The church is confronted not only by a task of great magnitude but also one of complexity. The competition for the time and attention of this generation is sterner, more subtle, and demands more of the church than in times past. Modern means of communication project vividly into our homes a bewildering variety of ideas and experiences. Many of these are good, and hold high promise as a means of furthering the teaching ministry of the church. Others, unfortunately, engender fears, uncertainties, prejudices, distorted values, moral laxities, and abet those subtle perversions which make evil glamorous and socially acceptable. The rising tide of juvenile delinquency indicates the seriousness of the present situation. In the words of Saint Paul as he faced the culture of Ephesus we say: "A wide door for effective work has opened to me, and there are many adversaries."[3]

The attractive surroundings with which our children

and youth are environed while in public school, and the great variety of interesting activities which make up the curricula of these institutions, lend further incentives to the church to provide facilities and procedures which do not suffer by comparison. Failure to meet this challenge puts religious teaching at a serious disadvantage, and adversely conditions even the best efforts of the church teaching staff.

To cope with these factors, the church needs to reevaluate her buildings, equipment, curricula, and her teaching procedures. The religious life and the hope of a better world are largely in the keeping of those who teach within the church. No other human institution can be expected to meet this solemn responsibility.

Signs of Promise

The difficulties and immensities of the present situation are not without some heartening encouragement to the religious educator. The current religious awakening, and particularly the concern of the thousands of young parents for the religious nurture of their children, holds promise for the future. The unprecedented shift of population within the nation has tended to bring new ideas and new leadership into churches which otherwise might never have enjoyed this helpful stimulation.

Out of the fruitful background of the past, new methods and procedures are emerging in the field of Christian education. The current revision of curricula by several of the major denominations is further evidence of the never-ceasing effort to provide the best possible means with which to make true religion effective in daily life. Persons who have not kept close to these recent developments will do well to bring themselves abreast of the current trends. They have promising implications which affect appreciably the future planning of church buildings and the selection of equipment.

---

[1] J. Brierly, *Studies of the Soul.* (1903)
[2] Roy M. Pearson, "Get out of the Church," *Christian Century* Pulpit. (October, 1955)
[3] I Corinthians 16:9 (RSVB)

CHAPTER 2

Present Trends..

As previously indicated, the changing patterns of modern life invite new procedures in Christian education, as they have invited them in all areas of human endeavor. The adjustments called for are the price of progress, and arise out of an earnest search for better ways of furthering the teaching ministry of the church.

Larger Learning Groups

Today the trend is toward teaching boys and girls in groups of larger size than was true a few years ago. The recommended size of the group varies from eight to fifteen children in the nursery to a maximum of twenty-five in a primary or junior group. This means a room for each group of the above numbers. Boys and girls are grouped together as they are in the homes and in public schools. The teaching staff is organized with a lead teacher and helping teachers in each group. See Chapters VII to XI for detailed information.

The great variety of purposeful activities which characterize their working and learning together as a group affords pupils and teachers a shared experience in Christian living. Christian attitudes are engendered, adjustments to and appreciation of other persons are furthered; head, heart, and hand are employed in a number of ways to bring out the aptitudes and to develop the skills of each and all. Under the guidance, but not the domination of the leader and her assistants, the group learns to live the Christian life by living and working together within the classroom.

Most of the activities related to the particular group are carried on within the room assigned to them. It should be noted that the teachers work as a team within the room. The pupil load per teacher or leader is not necessarily increased over that of the individual small classroom with a teacher for each room.

Larger Classrooms

It is apparent that such learning experiences as we have been describing require rooms with sufficient floor space to permit considerable freedom of movement and a variety of activities. It is claimed that pupils actually learn only 10 per cent of what they hear, 50 per cent of what they see, and 90 per cent of what they do. Learning by doing—interested participation in planned purposeful activities—becomes increasingly important. This entails larger classrooms, but not necessarily larger buildings. Furthermore, this more ample space is needed to provide against the overcrowding, irritation, and overstimulation of pupils, so detrimental to their interest and attention.

The rooms thus envisioned are quite different from the traditional cell-like classrooms (8' x 10') grouped about a central departmental assembly room. These small rooms restricted teaching to such limited procedures as could be carried on while seated about a table in cramped quarters. The assembly room stood idle except for brief worship periods. Otherwise, it served as a glorified sort of hallway through which all traffic to the classrooms must necessarily pass. Such an arrangement of the floor space was inflexible and imposed arbitrary grouping and teaching procedures upon the church school. All of this strikingly differs from the standards of the public schools so familiar to modern children and youth. Detailed information concerning the latest recommended standards are set forth in Chapters VII-X, which follow.

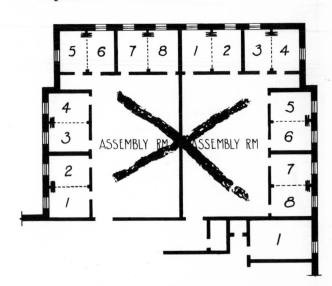

The Departmentally Arranged Educational Building

This represents a second stage in bringing the lesson material and the pupil together in terms of his needs and his own age group. Please note this arrangement is the Akron Plan carried over from the school as a whole to the department. Note the arbitrary arrangement of space and the definite restrictions placed upon teaching procedures by this and the Akron Plan.

Flexibility

Every effort is now being made when planning church school buildings to insure that direct access can be had to all rooms from a corridor or passageway. Thus every room can be used as needed without interfering with the work of other groups. By this accessibility and by keeping the rooms ample and varied in size, a large measure of flexibility in the use of space is made possible. Rooms can be reassigned as teaching procedures and pupil loads per room change from time to time.

The use of nonbearing, sound-controlling partitions between rooms permit further adjustments to meet changing conditions. These partitions can be taken out or restored as occasions demand with but slight marring of the building. Ample, movable storage cabinets, especially in classrooms, make possible ready access to a variety of equipment and the multiple use of these areas by different interest and age groups. Accessible storage space is a prime requisite for the modern church school building and the furtherance of the variety of activities which now attend the educational process.

Churches that wisely procure sites of adequate size can readily develop a master plan for their edifices which will permit building in units as needs for space arise and funds are available. Such a procedure permits a large measure of flexibility both in design and in satisfactory expansion of church school facilities to meet future needs.

Less Formality

Another observable trend commended by the leaders in the field of education is departure from formal worship centers for the children's departments of the church school. It is now felt that worship experiences which arise under the guidance of the leaders out of the actual teaching situation have much more meaning for children than the formal worship services in a departmental assembly room which have previously characterized our approach to children.

It is felt that a very simple worship center or corner within the room carefully planned with the children, and embellished with objects of significance to them, is more meaningful than the fixed and formal worship centers used in times past.

Informality in the worship and the general teaching procedures, which more and more is in evidence in the church school, does not imply that skillful guidance and careful planning are to be neglected. Rather, the informality is an attempt to give the children greater freedom, to bring more variety, and thereby to stimulate fresh interest.

Multiple Use of Space

There is a definite trend toward making multiple use of rooms and equipment in church school buildings. Dictated for the most part by necessity, and instituted in many instances over the opposition of those who are convinced that it won't work, once tried, it has worked surprisingly well.

In her article, "Did You Ever Have a Dream Cut in Half," *International Journal of Religious Education,* October, 1955, Frances N. Broadhurst states: "(1) By using our two-session church school plan we have, in effect, doubled our space; (2) there is a 20 per cent increase in church school attendance; (3) there is an increase in church attendance; (4) more people are involved in the teaching responsibility; (5) our classrooms are not overcrowded and teachers are set free to do more creative teaching than before; (6) families with small children responded wholeheartedly."

Briefly stated, such a program entails: (1) a patient, skillful enlistment of the church people and their willingness to give it a fair trial; (2) a careful scheduling and co-ordinating of church worship and church school sessions to enable all concerned to get to their appointed places on time and without confusion; (3) the training of additional teachers and officers and the enrollment of pupils for one or other of the church school sessions; (4) the designing of the church edifice as a whole to permit simultaneous use of the educational space and of the place of worship.

It will become evident at once that if such a program is undertaken, the church will need to exercise great care in planning the building. It might even involve adequate parking space with good exits and entrances leading to that much desired space. The control of distracting sound will be an important feature. Ample corridors and other features to which attention will be directed in later chapters will be involved.

Undertaken as an expedient, in many instances this multiple use of space has been permanently adopted. It permits better building space and equipment for available building dollars where funds are limited. It, apparently, meets a human need with gratifying results to the church as a whole.

Meeting Human Needs

Another trend which is coming more and more to the forefront, is the constant effort to discover the actual needs of persons at each stage of their growth and development. As a consequence, a greater variety of approaches are being made to the pupils of the church school.

In times past, the greater part of the religious nurture afforded by the church was carried forward in the formal sessions of the Sunday school. Today religious education has branched out to include a great many purposeful activities which are conducted not only on Sunday but during the weekday hours. The churches vary greatly in the programs which they feel are essential in their efforts to meet these human needs as they analyze their communities and seek to minister to them in terms of actual requirements rather than in terms of a stereotyped program.

Importance, therefore, is attached to the careful planning of the building to meet the requirements of each given situation. The installation of adequate storage space and the careful planning of the rooms make possible the use of each room for a great variety of undertakings. It is evident that the persons who assume the responsibility for planning a church building today need to be thoroughly familiar with the recent trends and with the actual needs of the church.

To provide sufficient floor space, while good in itself, is not enough. Rooms must have quality and character, and be designed and furnished to further the sacred work of the church in providing religious training and growth for all those who come within the church school building.

Recognition of the Importance of Environment

While there is no adequate substitute for a capable teacher implemented with a good curriculum, the surroundings in which the learning process takes place are very important. Environment is dynamic. It conditions the attitudes and responses of persons. Experiments carried on in industry, the public schools, and research clinics, stress the importance of the environmental factors in education. Children, in particular, are most sensitive to their surroundings. In the light of this, careful attention needs to be given to the selection of the fabrics and furnishings which go to make up the physical surroundings which condition the learning experience.

If the church has ample grounds landscaped to provide a lawn, attractive shrubs and flowers, then windows, low enough to permit children to view these evidences of God's handiwork, will add another worthwhile dimension to the classrooms. The God of growing things becomes more real and intimate especially to the younger children. Furthermore, this window view tends to overcome feelings of confinement and undue restriction so disturbing to the very young.

True, a wholesome environment is admittedly only a part of a total learning situation. Relatively speaking, it is so important that present day educators are giving it more and more attention with results that are gratifying. The church school can also lift the levels of attention and interest within its walls by taking thought concerning the little things which together make learning a delight as well as a discipline.

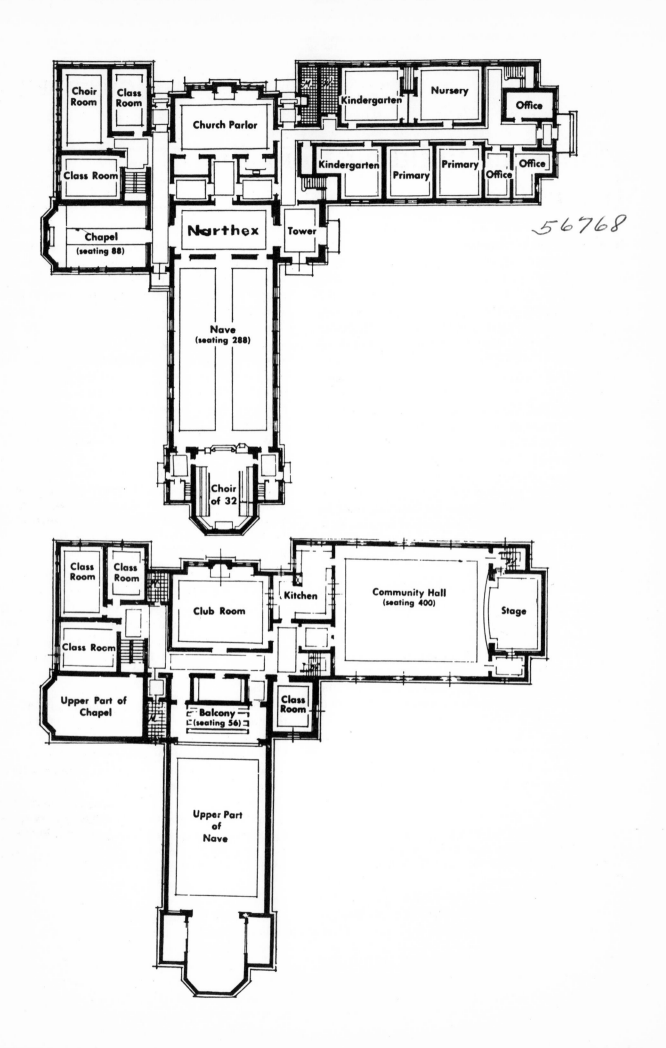

56768

CHAPTER 3

Plan Your Building from the Inside Out

Form Should Follow Function

An outwardly beautiful church building has much to commend it. As a consequence, church building committees far too often are more concerned with the outward appearance of the building than they are with the efficiency of the working spaces within it. It should be pointed out that buildings designed in traditional styles sometimes impose arbitrary arrangement of window space, of classroom walls, and even of passageways within the building. Such buildings, designed for procedures which are no longer adequate to meet the changing patterns of human life, impose serious handicaps on the teaching ministry of the church.

It is, therefore, important that the church carefully determine her strategy before busying herself with building plans or architectural style. The building, if it is to serve as it should its sacred function, must be planned to enclose the total program of the church in its forthgoing ministry. The place to begin planning a new church building is with the program that is to be enclosed by the walls and roof.

The backbone of a good educational building is a clearly conceived program of procedures to be carried on within its walls. A building erected around such a program will, in the hands of a skillful architect, be both efficient and pleasing in appearance. Such a building will lend itself to greater flexibility in use, and will permit constant adjustments to meet the changing requirements of the passing years. Plan your building, we say again, from the inside out. Let the form of the building follow the functions of your program of teaching and ministry.

It is unfortunate, in many instances, that those who wield a strong influence in the building program, do not view the entire enterprise with fair proportional interest for all its parts. Some churches, for example, will spend far more for a pipe organ, an elaborate tower, decorative trim, than they will for the church school equipment needed to make the religious teaching of the church effective. For this reason we say, first build a program geared to the religious needs of the community, and then plan the building to enclose the functions of the church.

Church Work Should Not Be Guesswork

In most situations where any considerable outlay is to be made for building purposes, a religious survey or census should be conducted to eliminate guesswork,

and to get needed facts for intelligent planning. Such a study or survey should include an appraisal of the services rendered by community social agencies in the church's area of responsibility, with a view to planning co-operatively for the welfare of the total community. Experience clearly indicates that even the church which has been long located in a given community should periodically re-evaluate her ministry. In new communities where growth and development are incomplete, and many basic facts unknown, it is imperative that church leaders make every effort to appraise both present and future demands for ministry.

While many churches will shirk this arduous work, they do so at their own peril. Surely, we can eliminate much of the unwise churchmanship of the past, and locate our churches and erect our buildings definitely related to actual needs rather than to vague surmises. When building for Christian education, the church leaders should have in hand the following basic information:

1. A clear statement of the teaching philosophy of the church and the denomination concerned.

2. A master plan covering the total requirements of the church and the church school.

3. A list of all Sunday and weekday activities of the church for each age group so multiple use of space may be carefully explored, and no needed space be omitted.

4. A statement showing the number of persons and their ages for whom the church is to provide space and equipment.

5. A statement of the rooms required in the light of present day religious educational standards to house adequately each age group.

6. A statement of the floor spaces required for each group to enable them to carry forward the program of the church. These should be in keeping with the standards set forth in subsequent chapters dealing with the needs of the age groups.

7. A list of the basic equipment for each teaching situation.

8. A study looking to the possible need for two or more sessions of the church school for each age group where funds and space are limited.

9. A study of the possible use of the facilities of community agencies to supplement those of the church with a view to effecting economies and engendering co-operative community relationships.

10. If the best methods are to be used and a larger program is expected with the completion of the new facilities, a teacher training program is necessary.

The success of a church building program rests ultimately with the congregation. Therefore, it is essential that the minister and the church building committee gain the support of the entire membership for such a project. Individual members should be convinced of the importance of good physical equipment for the furtherance of the religious program of their community. To do this, a careful planning and enlisting of church people will be required. Furthermore, publicity designed to carry the story of the church and its work and its needs to all the families of the constituency will be imperative.

While the tendency of many churches is to put members of the official boards of the church on the planning and building committee, we believe that it is essential to select the personnel for the planning and building committee because of personal qualities and aptitudes. Each of these persons should be chosen for specific pieces of work for which he is qualified and for which he has demonstrated ability. The church should not hesitate to infuse new blood into the working committees.

The plan of organization and the number of committees which we suggest will necessarily have to be modified in each local situation to meet and best to serve the requirements of that situation.

Before Building, Build a Working Organization

First, select a general chairman who should be a recognized leader and a capable executive who can inspire the co-operation of his associates. Next, determine the number of working committees you are going to need, and select the best possible chairman for each committee. Select committee personnel on the basis of ability and aptitude. The size and the number of committees should be determined by the size of the church membership and the nature of building operation. The general chairman, and the chairmen of the working committees will, together with the pastor, ex officio, comprise an executive committee or cabinet of what is to be known as the *Building Council*. This will facilitate the convening of committees and the screening of suggestions before passing suggestions on to the executive committee of the building council.

By sympathetically identifying themselves with the several organization of the church, the working committees can give these groups and their leaders a sense of being an integral and necessary part of the total program. Needs and valuable suggestions will be discovered. New ideas and the reasons for doing things can be shared. The building program will thus reach out to include the whole church constituency.

This cabinet or executive committee of the council as a whole, compiles the information and, after careful study, makes recommendations to the church for its approval. Wherever possible, avoid presenting alternative plans to an open meeting of the congregation. The following committees, together with their duties, are suggested:

THE BUILDING COUNCIL

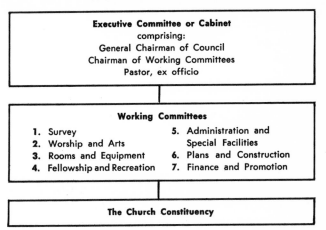

(Committees 2, 3, 4 will need to work together to avoid cross purposes.)

The Survey Committee Should

Conduct a religious census and/or a community survey, and thereby learn intimately the ages, the religious needs, and the church affiliations of the people in the church's area of responsibility; locate on a map the present membership and the possible future constituency; study the government census tracts, the projected population studies of the public utility companies and the public school officials for the local community. The Bureau of Research and Survey of the National Council of Churches, your state or local council of churches, and your denomination can give valuable guidance in appraising the results of the survey.

The Committee on Worship and the Arts Should

Evaluate present trends in meeting the worship requirements of each age group, generally determine what makes this experience most meaningful at each age level, and recommend pictures, works of art, and such equipment as will assure maximum effectiveness.

The Committee on Rooms and Equipment Should

Study pertinent publications of the several denominations and of the Division of Christian Education of the National Council of Churches and, in conference with the leaders in each department of the church's educational organization, recommend the rooms and equipment required for the total educational program of the church. In many instances, it will be found advisable to subdivide this committee and assign specialized studies to these smaller committees. Special attention should be given to audio-visual education requirements, multiple use of rooms, weekday and vacation church school needs.

The Committee on Fellowship and Recreation Should

Plan for the social, dramatic, indoor and outdoor recreational needs of the church, and thereby enhance and enlarge the church's outreach in ministry to the community.

Inasmuch as the dining hall, kitchen, parlor furnishings, game rooms, craft, hobby, and Scout rooms and kitchenette facilities are used by the whole church and are definitely related to the total program of Christian education, these should receive particular attention, and should be closely integrated with the findings of the Committee on Christian Education.

The Committee on Administration and Special Facilities Should

Make recommendations concerning adequate space and equipment for church offices, pastor's study and conference rooms, church board meeting places, and rooms for other staff workers, and for the proper facilities, storage space, and workroom for the person caring for the church property.

Particular attention should be given to the mechanical installation of the building such as heating, lighting, ventilation, rest rooms and drinking fountains to insure their adequacy, proper location, and freedom from distracting sound interference. (See Chapter V.)

The Plans and Construction Committee Should

Investigate and recommend architectural service, investigate and, after approval of the architect, recommend contractors, study in conference with the architect the materials, mechanical equipment, etc., suitable for the church building under consideration, secure and exhibit tentative plans and estimates of costs of the proposed building as directed by the executive committee, and, when approved by the church, secure construction drawings and specifications, proceed with the erection of the building or any parts thereof, and work closely with the finance and promotion committees. This committee should designate one person to transmit all instruction to the architect in writing, and through the architect to the builders and, where necessary, appoint a subcommittee on landscaping.

The Committee on Finance and Promotion Should

After careful study and planning, recommend to the executive committee for final approval of the church, a program for procuring the needed building funds. The preparation of the publicity program to insure the intelligent co-operation of the church constituency is another important duty of this committee. Current literature on successful church building fund campaigns and conferences with experts in this field will be of great value to all concerned.

It may be well, in some instances, to appoint two committees for the work described above, namely, a Finance Committee, and a Promotion and Publicity Committee.

The program just outlined will demand a great deal of careful supervision. The chairman of each committee will need to make every effort to see that his committee assignments are carried out on time, and that the complete information required of them be furnished. If this program is followed in detail, and the church building program is carried into the homes of all the families in the constituency, the church building, when erected, will be the result of the sacrifice, the interest, and the planning of the entire church constituency. This is Christian education at its best, and will bear long-run, fruitful results, if carried through with courage and attention to detail.

CHAPTER 4

The Voice of Experience

The planning and erection of a building for Christian education is a complicated undertaking demanding the counsel of persons who have intimate knowledge of what is needed. Few, if any, members of the ordinary church building committee have ever taken part in the planning of such a structure. This is not surprising, inasmuch as a new church building or the major modifications of an existing building are seldom called for a second time within the lifetime of most church members.

An educational leader has recently said: "An architect may make mistakes in planning and in design. However, there are more errors committed by the educators through failure to establish proper statements of educational needs and through failure to determine policy and organization which are to be followed. It is easier to figure the stresses and strains of a building than it is to determine what will be wanted ten or fifteen years hence in educational policy and organization. Yet this does not excuse a superintendent from attempting scientifically to forecast what the situation will be in the church school. Formerly, the architect was the chief consultant in planning a school building. Now, the educational factors should have the right of way over the architecture. The standpoint of educational needs comes first."[1]

To avoid costly mistakes and designing a building inadequate for the requirements of the church, the Building Committee is well advised to seek the services of those agencies who specialize in the planning of church facilities.

Professional Consultants

More and more churches are making use of the services of a professional consultant. The service he renders is needed far in advance of the work of the architect. Such service prepares the way for the qualified church designer. The qualified consultant helps church members to survey their needs. He brings them into contact with the best practices in church work, and helps them to develop a suitable program for their community. The consultant is not an architect, his work is not to be confused with that of the very important and frequently essential work of a *consulting* architect.

The building consultant gives guidance and advice regarding such items as how to (1) organize the building enterprise, (2) to determine the needs in view of population trends and changes, (3) to evaluate and possibly improve the present methods and program of the local church, (4) to select the architectural service for a given project, (5) to assemble a statement of requirements as to rooms, floor areas, equipment, et cetera needed, and (6) how to organize the financial and promotional program, perhaps with the aid of specialists in church finance. Guidance in these and related matters can save a great deal of time, money, and energy.

Many of the Protestant denominations provide building advice through their church erection boards, departments of Christian education, useful publications, and field consultants.

There are experienced and competent directors of Christian education in churches who have kept abreast of recent trends in Christian education and, in many instances, have served their churches when education buildings have been erected. Persons with such a background can be of assistance where building programs are in progress.

There are competent architects who are sympathetic and conversant with the general requirements of Christian education. Many of these architects devote themselves almost exclusively to church building, and make it a point to sit in on all important conferences whereby they keep in touch with the very latest developments in churchmanship. The Bureau of Church Building is always ready to provide a list of architects in different parts of the country who have shown an aptitude for and a sympathetic interest in church design.

The National Council of the Churches of Christ in the United States of America through conferences and literature on church building makes available to inquiring churches a most valuable service.

The Division of Christian Education of the National Council of Churches is staffed with persons who have devoted years of study to the specialized needs of each of the age groups of the church. Through their literature, workshops, and conferences, they provide a wide variety of helpful guidance.

The Bureau of Research and Survey of the National Council of Churches, while it cannot hope to carry on all the requested surveys of local situations, can supply guidance and helpful information.

Many of the state, county, and city councils of churches have trained research and survey people on their staffs who can render valuable service in organizing churches for surveys and religious census undertakings. Their expert appraisal of the facts thus gathered proves most helpful to the church needing this type of service.

Many churches hesitate to make even minor expenditures for such counsel as we have mentioned. With some measure of justification, they may resent what they feel is outside interference in their building plans. Nevertheless they will be doing themselves a disservice if they do not avail themselves of information and counseling services available.

Once the building is erected, it is costly to modify the structure. It is even more costly to work in that structure over a long period of years, if it is poorly planned, and does not serve the purposes for which the funds were given. Nothing is so dampening to the enthusiasm of a church after a considerable sacrificial financial outlay as the realization that they have made serious, needless mistakes in planning their building. On the other hand, an attractive, adequate, well planned building is both an inspiration and a fitting instrument with which to further the ministry of the church.

---

[1] Source unknown

CHAPTER 5

Usable and Livable.

The church school building houses a great variety of activities, and ministers to persons of all ages. For these reasons building plans should give attention, not only to the structural and mechanical adequacy of the building, its appearance, cost, etc., but also to the health, safety, comfort, convenience, and happiness of the people who come within its walls. How these people feel and react has an important bearing upon the effectiveness of the church's ministry.

If people are comfortable, and find the facilities convenient, and go away with a sense of satisfaction, they undoubtedly will wish to return. On the other hand, particularly small children, if they are frightened by their first entrance into the church building where they are confronted with dark, forbidding corridors, strange institutional odors, and drab surroundings, will react unfavorably. Both parents and teachers will experience some difficulty in persuading them to return of their own volition. The building needs to be livable as well as usable.

Briefly, here are some of the general considerations which, if carefully provided for, will make the building more satisfactory in every way.

Circulation

One of the basic considerations in planning a church school building is to make sure that persons can have ready access to the building, and that they can pass from the entrance to their particular room without having to pass through any other working space. Likewise, it is important that all rest rooms and other special areas of the building to which the public should have access, can be readily reached from the central hallways.

This problem of adequate circulation involves steps, doorways, corridors, and stairways. Inasmuch as both very young children and older adults make use of the church facilities, it is important to keep outside steps to the minimum. Wherever possible, the entrances to the church school building should be near or on grade level.

Steps on the inside of the building can be kept to the minimum by keeping the ceiling heights to 8 feet 6 inches or 9 feet. This will cut down the height of the stairs to be climbed, and will contribute to lowering the cost of construction. Care should be taken to keep the risers low, the treads wide, and to see to it that all steps and stairways are well lighted. In most instances, a handrail on either side of the steps is required by most building codes as a safety measure.

Care should be exercised to eliminate all winding stairways or angled steps. Wherever possible, eliminate a combination of two steps. Apparently persons will stumble over a single step, and recover their balance, but the accidents on a two-step combination are usually many and severe. Three steps are usually seen in time to prevent accidents, and are much safer.

Corridors and stairways are subjected to a great deal of traffic and consequent wear. It is important that floors, stair treads and risers, and walls be constructed of materials which are impervious to scuffing, scratching, and marring. While the subject of acoustics will be treated at length in a subsequent paragraph, we emphasize the special need for sound control in all corridors.

Partitions and Doors

The construction of wall partitions and the installation of doors should be given careful study. Partitions should eliminate sound and sight disturbances, and present a smooth surfaced wall which can be readily cleaned, decorated, and maintained. Wherever possible, partitions should be nonbearing. This is particularly true between classrooms. Nonbearing partitions make possible greater flexibility in the realignment of space as requirements change from time to time. (See Chapter II, section on "Flexibility.")

Walls within classrooms and in corridors should be free from sharp angles and projections. At least one wall in every classroom should be unbroken and free from doors, windows, chalkboards or any other built-in equipment.

The placement of doors and the quality of materials used are important. If a door is of flimsy construction, a great deal of the sound from the corridors will pass into the classrooms. This will cut down the teaching efficiency of the classrooms. The placement of doors should be studied for each classroom to determine just where they should be placed with respect to a specific room, and also with reference to other rooms across the corridor. Wherever possible, doors should be so placed that they do not cause congestion in the corridor or hallway immediately adjacent.

Classrooms

It is recommended that classrooms have the general proportion of 3 feet in width to each 4 feet of length, or 4 feet to 5 feet. Where possible, the classrooms should be placed the long way of the outside wall so as to permit the maximum window space.

There should be no posts or jutting walls to break up the classroom floor space and to make it difficult to plan or carry on the activities essential to the teaching process.

Every effort should be made to eliminate any interior rooms, that is, rooms that have no outside exposure. In any case, small children should not be placed in such areas. The same is true of basement areas. Children should not be put in rooms that are below ground level except in a few instances where the floors are not more than 3 feet below grade and preferably are heated with panel heating installations to ensure a warm floor surface.

It is well, in planning classrooms, to make certain that there are no small or restricted rooms (i.e., 8'0" x 10'0"). Rooms should be of various sizes so as to provide greater flexibility of space use to meet the changing needs of the years.

Windows

Windows in educational rooms should be of clear, unobstructed glass, and should equal in area not less than 18 to 25 per cent of the floor space of a given room.

In the space used by small children, the window sills should be low enough to permit the children to see the out-of-doors. Care should be taken to place the window area at the side and the rear of the room so as not to have direct light shining into the eyes of the pupils.

If apertures are made in the windows for ventilation, these openings should be shielded so as not to induce drafts within the room.

Floors

Floor surfaces are an important part of the church building, particularly in the children's areas where they are accustomed to sit and to play and to work on the floors. Generally speaking, churches need to give careful attention to the materials and color schemes selected for the floor surfaces of their buildings. A good floor surface stands up well under constant wear, is readily cleaned, and gives character to the room or area in which it is located.

Flooring and floor covering should be selected for beauty, durability, restfulness, and ease in maintenance. Floors should be attractive, suitable, but not conspicuous. Distinct designs in floor coverings are to be avoided.

Floors made of hardwood properly finished, remain attractive if they are carefully maintained. There is no wood finish that will stand up under the wear of gritty shoes and classroom furniture without frequent treatment. The importance of quiet and soundproofing should be kept in mind when selecting floors and floor coverings. Sound affects not only the person within the given classroom, but if the room is on an upper story, the type of floor surface has considerable bearing upon the sound conditions that exist in the room beneath.

Concrete floors above ground level should be covered with linoleum, cork, rubber, vinyl, or asphalt tile, or some other composition suitable to be placed over a concrete surface. Linoleum and wooden floor coverings do not stand up well in damp, basement areas; asphalt tile is recommended.

Tile flooring is sanitary, easily cleaned, and requires no expensive upkeep. It may be had in appropriate dark green, brown, and other plain or various tile effects. Linoleum, with its unlimited range of colors, affords a great deal of variety. Linoleum, battleship $\frac{3}{16}$-inch thickness, has long wearing qualities. Rubber tile, a bit more expensive than linoleum, has excellent wearing qualities, tends to lessen the noise intensity, has great resiliency, and a wide range of decorative colors and designs.

Plastic tile coverings are coming on the market in greater volume, and are proving acceptable. They are durable, sanitary, and have definite color possibilities.

Cork tile and cork floorings are quiet and comfortable, have excellent insulating qualities, some acoustical value, and are less slippery than most floor materials.

Asphalt tile is probably the most widely used floor covering, especially where the church budget is a bit restricted. Tiles can be applied over concrete floors in basements or over old wooden floors. Asphalt tile, however, should not be laid on wood floors or on cement or grade floors without a sealer coat.

As previously stated, floor levels for children's rooms should be above outside grade level, and in no case in a basement which is more than 3 feet below grade. Care should be exercised to see that these surfaces are warm enough so the children can sit and play on them without incurring a health hazard.

Toilet Facilities

	Washbasin	Toilet Stool
Nursery children	24" from floor	10" from floor
Kindergarten children	26" from floor	12" from floor
Primary children	28" from floor	14" from floor
Junior children	30" from floor	16" from floor

Toilet Facilities

While the demand upon these facilities is not as great in the church school building as in public schools, ample provisions should be made for proper toilet rooms for both sexes on each floor. By good planning, these installations can be placed adjacent to each other and stacked perpendicularly, where there is more than one story, and thereby keep down the cost of the building.

These facilities should be well ventilated and lighted, and finished in sanitary material such as tile or well painted plaster wall surfaces.

In most instances, separate provision should be made for the young children. Their toilet rooms should open directly into or be very near their rooms. These toilets should be equipped with juvenile fixtures. If adult fixtures are used, portable wooden steps should be provided to care for the smaller children.

It is well to label the doors of the children's toilets, both by clearly printed inscription, and supplement the same with a picture indicating that one room is for boys and the other for girls.

The doors of the male and female toilets should not be within sight of each other. They should be accessible and clearly marked.

Heating, Ventilating, and Air Conditioning

The effectiveness of the Christian education building is very greatly conditioned by the heating and ventilating and air conditioning systems. Extremes of temperature, lack of fresh air, drafts and noise arising from improperly installed mechanical equipment, can disrupt the teaching efficiency of any school.

All heating outlets such as radiators should be shielded for the protection of children.

The choice of a particular heating system, ventilating equipment, and air conditioning equipment is a matter which requires expert advice. Instances have been brought to our attention where high pressure salesmen have sold churches pieces of equipment which, when installed, proved to be under capacity, generally unsatisfactory, and noisy. We suggest that you deal only with competent architects and engineers specializing in these fields.

Now that air conditioning is becoming more general in use in parts of the country requiring it, churches should be cautious in their selection of such equipment. Great care should be taken to make certain that the pumps and compressors are placed away from the interior of the building. The noise necessarily generated by these pieces of equipment can be a disturbing factor in a church building. Air conditioning, apparently, is here to stay, and with the passing of the years, is becoming more efficient and better adapted to church use. Churches that have installed such equipment commend it both for the comfort it affords, and for the better attendance maintained during the hot seasons of the year.

Lighting and Electrical Installations

The well-being, comfort, and attention levels of pupils are greatly affected by the control and adequacy of light. The intensity of the light in any given

room also affects the color scheme with which the areas are decorated. For this reason, the lighting and decorating should be preferably in the hands of the architect who can co-ordinate the various factors, and produce a pleasing and a functionally satisfactory result.

Light switches should be conveniently placed, and free from noise or distraction in operation. Make certain that outlets for the many electrical devices are properly placed in each room.

Now that audio-visuals are being used increasingly, it is important that the proper kind of wiring be installed, speakers be placed in the right positions for good sound effects, and that outlets be so placed that projectors can be operated without running electrical cords across the areas where persons must walk. (See Chapter XI.)

Where pictures are to be projected in daylight, proper window coverings in keeping with the decorative scheme of the room should be installed.

Not only should light be provided and regulated in the proper intensities as measured in foot candles in teaching areas, but caution should be taken to control the outside light as well as that emanating from the fixtures.

All of these matters are quite beyond the amateur or the average building committee, and should be carefully studied with the architect as a co-ordinator of the several experts required to get a satisfactory result.

Hats and Coats

To prevent crowding, confusion, irritations, and to further the general well-being, ample provision should be made to place storage areas for hats and coats convenient to the classrooms. Generally speaking, it has been found advisable for the persons above primary age to place hat and coat storage along the corridor walls. Preferably, these storage spaces should be recessed, and of sufficient depth to permit the coat hanger to be suspended from a rod, and of sufficient

Space for Wraps
Always protect children from hooks. This may be done by placing a shelf for caps and hats above the hooks.

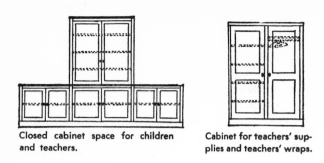

Closed cabinet space for children and teachers.

Cabinet for teachers' supplies and teachers' wraps.

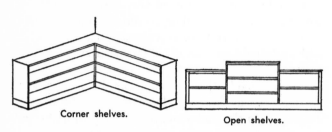

Corner shelves.

Open shelves.

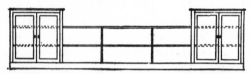

Open shelves with closed space for teachers' supplies at either end.

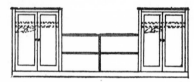

Open shelves with place for children's wraps at either end.

From Equipment and Arrangement for Children's Groups in the Church, **Emma Jane Kramer.** Used by permission.

length to take care of the needs of the pupils in the adjacent areas. Make certain that if occasional coat hooks are used these are shielded by a shelf so there is no danger of these sharp projections injuring the eyes of the pupils.

The storage spaces should be designed as to height to meet the requirements of the different age groups. If storage space for overshoes is provided at the bottom of the cabinet and a shelf at the top for hats, coats on hangers can be stored at intervals of three inches and a very considerable number of them put into a small space.

Attention should be given to the proper ventilation of these storage areas, particularly in damp weather.

Walk-in cloak closets are not recommended. Younger pupils engage in pushing and shoving to get access to their wraps. Older persons find these rooms become congested while persons are trying to locate their belongings. In most instances, these areas are not well ventilated, are poorly lighted, and generally form a bottleneck in cold or rainy weather.

In the nursery, kindergarten, and primary departments, it is best to have the coat and hat storage cabinets within the classroom areas. This permits the teachers to assist the smaller children with their wraps, and shields the children from the pushing and confusion which are liable to result if these small children make use of the corridor coat storage space.

Storage

Reference has previously been made to the importance of providing ample storage cabinets throughout the entire educational building. If church buildings lack one thing above another, it is adequate facilities for storing the many kinds of equipment used by a church. To make sure that sufficient provision is made for storage, every working unit of the church should be requested to enumerate in detail the materials and equipment which they need to store. Such a list will include the machines and materials required by the building caretaker as well as the many adult working organizations.

It is recommended that, when figuring floor space for classrooms, 10 per cent extra footage be included to assure ample storage space without cutting into the needed floor areas assigned to teaching purposes.

Walk-in storage closets are not recommended. They usually become catch-alls for materials. Free standing cabinets are much better. They can be specifically designed for the requirements of a given room and, if necessary, can be moved from one room or area to another.

Drinking Fountain
Recessed in the Wall and at the Proper Height.

Drinking Fountains

Drinking fountains should be placed where they can be easily reached, preferably recessed in the wall. They should be in close proximity to the plumbing installation leading to the toilet facilities, thereby to reduce the cost on installation. Select fountains which are suitable for all ages and in which the water flow is controlled so the children cannot damage their clothing or the building by splashing the water. Fountains should be placed at proper height so small children can reach them readily. When standing at the sink, the top should be a little below the children's hips. If all fountains are placed at one height for adult use, a step should be placed around these adult installations so they can also be used by the young children. Many school authorities recommend that the same procedure be followed in installing toilet facilities. It is easier to install or to remove a low step which will permit the use of adult fixtures than to make the necessary plumbing changes, if room areas are reassigned.

Acoustics

The control of disturbing sounds within the educational building, has much to do with its usability and "livability." Sounds of annoying intensity may be generated within the teaching areas, or they may originate outside the classroom and be transmitted through walls, floors, doors, or other openings such as heating and ventilating ducts, and transoms. In any case, such distractions can be readily controlled. Acoustics is an exact science today. Improper control of excessive sound is inexcusable.

Bad acoustics result from the repeated reverberation of the original sounds emanating from the human voice or a musical instrument which bounce around the room from one hard surface to another. This is particularly acute in rooms with cement floors, large undraped windows, and high gloss varnish paint on walls and ceiling. Acoustical tile, travertine tile, or acoustical plaster on ceilings, window draperies, and carpets can be used to correct existing bad conditions. Such bad conditions should not characterize a building designed by a competent architect.

It is advisable that all corridors be acoustically treated and that classroom doors and walls be so constructed as to shut out sound originating in hallways, stair wells, and conference areas. Likewise, care should be exercised to insure that all mechanical contrivances within the building are so located and insulated as to eliminate noise nuisances emanating from them.

It hardly seems necessary, in this day and generation, to stress this subject of acoustics. Yet all too frequently we find new buildings plagued by inadequate sound control with consequent unnecessary lowering of interest, attention, and comfort.

CHAPTER 6

Light and Color

Recognition of the importance of adequate lighting, and particularly the value of color in classrooms is a recent development. It is now known that together they have an appreciable physical and psychological effect upon human behavior. The comfort, attention levels and conduct of pupils are definitely conditioned by light and color. A well decorated room possesses charm, a sense of pleasurable welcome, and by its attractiveness stimulates the desire to return to it again.

Meaningful religious experiences are more likely to be engendered in surroundings which afford a sense of satisfaction, elevate the mind, and invite the cheerful participation of the pupils. The church that dismisses these factors as being of little importance, or fails to plan for their skillful use, will undoubtedly pay a heavy price in lowered efficiency within her classrooms. Relatively speaking, good lighting and purposeful use of color do not make excessive demands upon the church building dollars. A modest financial outlay, "know-how," and intelligent planning for the building as a whole, can give a new look to an old building, and lend charm and grace to a new structure.

Together

Light and color should be planned together, and determined ultimately by actual application within each room. Three considerations make this necessary: (1) the intensity and the quality of light vary more or less in each room according to its outside exposure, the size of the windows, and the lighting system; (2) the intensity and the quality of the light conditions appreciably the value of colors within a given room. For example, it has been demonstrated that an incandescent light gives a gray wall a slightly reddish appearance. A daylight fluorescent lamp gives a blue appearance, and a soft, white fluorescent lamp produces a green appearance. Daylight of varying intensities also modifies color value within a room. (3) Color on wall surfaces, floors and ceiling affects the light that impinges upon them. Heavy dark colors tend to absorb the light, and give less than 30 per cent of it back into the working spaces of the room. On the other hand, very light colors give back sometimes 70 per cent of all the light falling upon them.

Under the first set of circumstances, the room will be dull, drab, and disappointing. Under the second set of circumstances, the light may tend to "bounce" around the room and, if too intense, to produce discomfort and fatigue due to eye strain. In either case

the result is not satisfactory. Where pupils suffer from eye discomfiture, either through squinting or the uneven focusing of the eyes upon work, serious and harmful conditions are induced. We are dealing here with the physics and the physiology of light and color. They are measurable and important. They definitely affect people psychologically.

With a Purpose and a Plan

In a recent unpublished manuscript, T. Norman Mansell, architect, reminds us, "Man is affected emotionally by color as by music, and most people are affected far more by the color of their surroundings than they realize. Beautiful color is a poem of silent music as effective with some of us as a quiet prayer."[1]

Yes, color and light have their psychological effects. It is therefore important to establish just what we desire to elicit from the persons who occupy our classrooms. Is the particular room to invite dignity, reverence, and meditation or should it be cheerful, light, stimulating, or utilitarian? In answering this question, we need to determine what the purpose of the classroom is and then, with the best judgment, to bring these two powerful allies of color and light to our assistance.

Such purposeful planning as we suggest should be geared to the needs of the people of each age level who will occupy the several classrooms. Furthermore, it will include the careful selection of all of the factors which go to give the room character. We will need to take into consideration the floor surfaces, the wall, the ceiling, the woodwork, the draperies at the window, furniture, cabinets, and wood trim.

What we suggest for each individual room should also be a governing principle for the building as a whole. Consideration should be given to the basic color of one room as related to the room next to it and to the visual effect of the transition from one room to another. Such planning will mitigate against monotony, and assure a pleasing variety of color schemes which will give a building a sparkle and an interest which otherwise might be overlooked.

Such planning, we hope, will deliver the church from the personal tastes of those individuals whose unfortunate color preferences or desires for utility work to the decided disadvantage of good interior decoration.

Which Colors?

There is no infallible color formula which can be

applied in all situations. The test must be made in the room itself with due consideration for the people who live and work in it. The effect of the same color combination will vary in different rooms, depending upon the natural or artificial light entering the room, the finish of the wall surfaces, and the way the paint is applied.

As a general rule, soft, mellow pastel shades should be chosen for wall surfaces and strong colors such as red, blue, and strong yellow should be avoided as being too stimulating. The warmer sunshine but not gaudy shades of yellow and buff may well feature rooms with a northern exposure. Rooms receiving a great deal of natural light require calming, cooling colors such as apple green, blue green, light olive, tea, or tones of gray. Pure white, because of its coldness, is not recommended for general use except for ceilings, where its high light-reflecting qualities help to reflect the light upon the working areas of the room. Some color authorities recommend extending the white of the ceiling down on the walls of the room a distance of about twelve to eighteen inches to insure an even and wide distribution of reflected light.

In his article, "Color in Schools," *Church Property Administration*, September-October, 1953, James D. McConnell suggests selection of the following colors: For schools: "Classrooms, east and north—warm colors (yellow, buff, warm red); west and south classrooms —cool colors; corridors, colors high in reflectiveness; offices—personal choice; (dark and rich colors can be used here); science rooms—low chroma, nondramatic colors (greens); library—light green; music rooms, peach or dusty rose; home economics rooms—ivory or buff; cafeterias—turquoise or warm peach; auditoriums —ivory, peach, or green."

The use of cheerful, predominantly neutral shades of flat paint provide a fitting wall background against which spots of beauty, color, and brightness can be accented without the discomfiture of too strong color contrasts. The judicious use of draperies, pictures, pottery, fabrics, murals, flowers, and plants will permit occasional or seasonal change of room decor without the expense of complete redecoration. Neutrally stained woodwork or good quality natural wood, finished with glossless varnish, lacquer, or wax, should characterize the cabinets, furniture, doors, and wood trim. Care should be taken to avoid the "busy" effect and overemphasis of the wood trim resulting from the use of strong, contrasting colors. Surfaces finished as we have indicated are readily cleaned, will not mar easily, and provide a neutral background for the furtherance of the decoration scheme which we have just described.

Now that classrooms are used for a variety of purposeful activities, and pupils are not oriented toward a particular wall area, there is little occasion for giving any wall surface a special color treatment to emphasize its focal importance. It is better, except in special instances, to use the same color for all walls within a given room. This permits a greater flexibility in the use of the room and the arrangement of the furnishings.

Generally Speaking

1. Never apply paint to good natural wood. Only wood of poor quality needs to be painted.

2. Avoid strong colors on large wall areas.

3. Avoid a variety of strong colors in one room. A pleasing variety can be found in the use of blending shades of one color or, at most, by the use of the blending of shades of two colors.

4. Avoid use of high gloss paints and varnishes except in special rooms where sanitation is the prime consideration.

5. Avoid putting strong or contrasting colors for blackness, brightness, contrasts, too close together. Such strong contrasts cause eye fatigue and lower pupil attention.

6. Test your colors on the wall and not by the use of a color card.

7. Make certain that the light is of the right intensity in terms of foot candles at the eye level of the pupils, and that the light is evenly distributed and adjusted to the requirements of the particular age groups and the activities carried on within a given room. Older persons need more light. Craft shops and fine work need special lighting. Avoid glare from windows and fixtures, and see to it that there are no dark areas within the room due to uneven distribution of light.

8. Plan the decoration of the whole building including walls, ceiling, furnishings, woodwork, and floor surfaces. Plan each room with all of these details in mind. Put the details for the whole building into a master plan so you may produce a varied and interesting building and avoid monotony.

9. Use your architect and possibly a professionally trained competent interior decorator to help with the planning. Color is dynamic. Make certain that you use it skillfully to bring beauty, joy, satisfaction, and effectiveness to your teaching experiences.

10. Put an item in the church budget which will permit a continuous upkeep of your building so the initial charm and grace may not be lost through poor housekeeping or gross neglect. A planned program which assures some work being done each year will avoid the necessity of raising an appreciable sum after a long period of deterioration. Someone has wisely said, "The proper study of mankind is man." It is the church's privilege to know what the pupil really needs in the way of color and light, and then to design the classrooms to meet this human need.

---

[1] T. Norman Mansell, "Color in the Church," Bureau of Church Building, National Council of Churches

CHAPTER 7

Grouping and Grading

Principles of Grading

God in his wisdom and love has made us growing persons. The church should identify itself understandingly with God's laws of growth inherent in human life, and thereby meet the spiritual needs of growing persons. While in some quarters there is a tendency to impose arbitrary adult conceptions on the minds of little children, for the most part we are approaching the task of Christian education with greater reverence for individual needs, aptitudes, and interests, and are endeavoring to understand exactly how God works in these unfolding personalities.

The fullest possible spiritual development of each individual at the level of his growth should be one of the major considerations of the church, and should determine the size of the groups and the grading system. While certain programs for grading and grouping generally prevail, it is important that each church school should carefully study its own situation. The size of the school, the number of persons at each age level, the groupings in which the children are placed in their public schools, the church school facilities, and the number of skilled teachers available, the time afforded for and the nature of the Christian education program offered, should be taken into consideration.

Every effort should be made to group pupils in such a way as to bring children of the same age, capacities, and interests together for their learning experiences, and to provide suitable space free from interruption.

In churches where the average attendance is not sufficient to provide a good working group or groups for each age level, it may be necessary to make the age span more inclusive than otherwise. In churches with larger average attendance where there are sufficient pupils to provide a good working group for each grade, a room or rooms should be provided for each group. Care should be taken to see that the number of pupils per teaching situation and the square footage per pupil are in keeping with the recommended standards.

Ways of Grouping and Grading

A more detailed description of the several ways of grouping and grading pupils in a particular church school can best be ascertained from the leaders and the publications on administration made available through your own denominational board on Christian education. It is important that this matter be determined early in the planning of the church school building, for it carries with it many factors affecting the layout of the floor areas and the teaching procedures which can

be employed. A school which insists upon the traditional assembly room with satellite small classrooms centered about it is bound to have an arrangement of floor areas and enclosing partitions differing substantially from the school which follows the newer approved methods with fewer but larger rooms.

Emphasis needs to be placed upon the importance of appraising not only the present requirements of the school as to teaching patterns, numbers of pupils per room, etc., but also upon the changes which the future may present. Today's influx of very young children will need to be reckoned with in the youth groups of some years hence. The projected population figures of your public school department will undoubtedly afford some guidance at this point.

In his approved manual, *Christian Nurture Through the Church,* Lee J. Gable gives (1) "The Traditional Departments of the Church School," and some helpful comments on grouping adults, and (2) "Adaptations Because of Size," which we quote with a slight adaptation of his chart on grouping.

"The Traditional Departments

The divisions and departments that have been commonly accepted in the Sunday church school are these:

Children's Division

Nursery Department	Under 4 years
Kindergarten Department	Ages 4, 5
Primary Department	Grades 1, 2, 3
Junior Department	Grades 4, 5, 6

Youth Division

Junior High Department	Grades 7, 8, 9
Senior High Department	Grades 10, 11, 12
Post High Department	High school graduation to young adulthood

Adult Division

Young Adults	Bases indicated below
Adults	Divided according to age
Older Adults	or interest

"The basis for grading is clear in each department through the senior high. Difficulty does not arise often in grading children and youth.

"There is no one basis for deciding when a person should enter or leave the young adult department. A person becomes a young adult gradually. It is usually agreed that a person should enter a young adult group when he has had three or four of the following 'transition experiences': leaving school, achieving self-support, marriage, leaving the parental home, reaching voting age, discharge from military service.

"Logically, we should establish graded classes for adults as we do for children and we should promote people from one group to another when they reach a given point in age or experience. Practically, however, this is difficult to do. There are no neat dividing lines for adults. And besides, many adults resent a grouping which is imposed on them.

"Adult grouping usually becomes a problem in the church when young adults feel that existing adult groups are 'too old' for them. The most practical solution is to start a new young adult group when this happens. The existing adult groups continue. Now and then it becomes possible to combine two or more of the older classes. This seems like a haphazard method, but it works fairly well.

"Another solution is to divide adult groups according to interest rather than age. This method should be more widely used as there is much to commend it. Let the church school set up an elective curriculum for adults, with choices that are varied enough to appeal to different interests and numerous enough to make classes of manageable size. These groups remain together only until the courses are completed, and then a new election of courses creates new groups. The social needs of people may be met through some type of continuing organization, perhaps the usual men's and women's organizations of the church."

"Adaptations Because of Size

"Most churches do not have eight different departments, each with its separate meeting place. They lack either the numbers of people or the space or both. They find it necessary to make some kind of combination. Combinations range all the way from four classes in a one-room church to the separate department for each grade which the large church may require.

"A chart suggesting various combinations of grouping is reproduced here from the *International Journal of Religious Education*.

"Even the smallest church should have the four groups suggested in the first line of the chart. The larger church will find the desired combination of groups farther down in the chart. Large churches may have a separate group for *each year or school grade*."

Two-grade Departments

"Children's workers remind us that there is considerable difference between the first-grader and the third-grader. It is very difficult for the primary department worker to challenge the one and be understood by the other at the same time. The same difference exists in the junior department between the fourth and sixth grades. There is no problem for each school grade. But what about the average and small churches?"[1]

There is a definite trend toward two-grade departments as the answer to the problem of the average or the small church. It provides a primary department or class consisting of grades one and two; a primary-junior department or class for grades three and four; and a junior department or class for grades five and six. Denominations which provide separate curriculum materials for the Primary-Junior department report large demand for it. New educational buildings in average small churches are increasingly providing for two-grade departments in the children's division, and in some cases in junior high and senior high departments.

SEVEN WAYS OF GROUPING

AGE GROUP				GRADES				AGE GROUP			
1.	Pre-school			Grades 1-6		Grades 7-12		Over 17			
2.	Pre-school			1-3	4-6	7-12		Over 17			
3.	Pre-school			1-3	4-6	7-9	10-12	Over 17			
4.	Under 4 years	4-5 years		1-3	4-6	7-9	10-12	Older Youth 18-23		Over 24	
5.	Under 3	3	4,5 Years	1-3	4-6	7-9	10-12	Older Youth 18-23	Young Adults 24-35	Over 35	
6.	Under 2	2	3	4, 5	1, 2	3, 4	5, 6	7-9	10-12	Older Youth 18-23	Young Adults 24-35	Adults 36-65	Older Adults Over 65
7.	Separate self-contained room or rooms for every grade										

Age-Group Expectancies

The following charts indicate for churches of various sizes the number of pupils per hundred total average attendance which may be expected (1) in each age group and (2) the rooms required in each instance.

The Presbyterian Church in the U.S.A. bases its findings on a sample survey dated 1950:[2]

Department	Average Enrollment per hundred pupils	
	All	Except Adults
Nursery	6	8
Kindergarten	12	17
Primary	18	25
Junior	15	21
Junior High	12	16
Senior	10	13
Young People (18-23 yrs.)	—	—
Adults (24 yrs. up)	27	—
Total	100	100

The Disciples of Christ, with an eye on what will happen in the next few years, have projected the following table:[3]

Group	Average per hundred pupils
Age 0-2	4
Age 3	4
Age 4-5	8
Primary—Age 6, 7, 8	12
Junior—Age 9, 10, 11	12
Junior High—Age 12, 13, 14	10½
Senior—15, 16, 17	9½
All others	40
Total	100 per cent

The General Board of Education of The Methodist Church has outlined the recommendations below:

"For guidance purposes in allocating floor space of different age levels, it is reasonable to anticipate an attendance in the respective departments of a church school approximately as follows:

Department	Percentage
Nursery	6-8
Kindergarten	8
Primary	12
Junior	12
Intermediate	11
Senior	10
Older Youth	5
Adult	35

"It should be emphasized that these percentages are general averages and that great variation may be found in different geographical areas.

"While these percentages are given as a general guide, it should not be assumed that they are applicable to all situations. Each church should carefully study its own population trends and make such adjustments as are necessary."[4]

It should be noted that the figures projected in the preceding charts are only approximate. Each church should carefully study its own constituency and the projected attendance figures of the public schools for a more accurate appraisal of building needs. (See Chapter III.)

These tables should also be studied in the light of Chapters VIII, IX, X, and XI.

---

1 Lee J. Gable, *Christian Nurture Through the Church,* (National Council of Churches, 1955)
2 Unpublished statement, Board of Christian Education, Presbyterian Church in the U.S.A.
3 Disciples of Christ, International Convention
4 Recommendations, General Board of Education, The Methodist Church.

CHAPTER 8

Meeting the Needs of the Preschool Children

Who Are They?

This group includes children from birth to five years of age inclusive. Generally speaking, they are classified as follows:

Birth to 2 years of age—Nursery I
2 years of age—Nursery II
3 years of age—Nursery III
4 years of age—Kindergarten I
5 years of age—Kindergarten II

Because of their tender, formative years, their special needs, and the far-reaching importance of this period in their religious development, these children should be objects of love, concern, and special consideration. What we do for and with them conditions appreciably the after years God may give them.

The very young (birth through two years—Nursery I and II)

In fairness to all concerned, it should be said that there is a difference of opinion as to the wisdom of committing children under three years of age to the care of the church school. For many, whose opinions are worthy of our respect, it is a matter of firm conviction that these very young children can be better cared for at home and should not be exposed to conditions usually obtaining in most of our church schools.

Other persons, concerned for the religious life of both parents and children, are equally firm in their insistence that the church should provide church care for these younger children to permit their parents to participate actively in the life of the church. Otherwise, there is always the possibility that two genera-

tions may miss the spiritual ministry of the church and even be lost to her life and service.

If the church accepts these youngest members of the fellowship, she should provide space for them, with such exact and loving care as to safeguard and further their physical and spiritual well-being.* Special provision should be made for their parents so they, too, may develop spiritually, understand how they can best foster the spiritual growth of their children and maintain a happy Christian home.

In these days when close co-operation between parents and the church is considered imperative for the fullest religious growth of all concerned, the church's best attention and efforts should be given to the solution of this problem. Halfway measures either in providing care or equipment are not worthy of the church, nor fair to the defenseless children.

Their Care

Wherever possible, the church should procure the services of a trained nurse with special aptitude for child care. Such a person may be a housewife not now engaged in her nursing profession. Associated with her will be as many assistants as circumstances may require.

Those who serve in the rooms for crib babies should be dressed appropriately in white uniforms, and should maintain hospital standards of sanitation, both personally and in the maintenance of the room and equipment.

These very young children are in need of special protection from infection, undue noise, overcrowding,

*See leaflets 2, 3, 4, and 5 for the Division of Christian Education, N.C.C.U.S.A.

overstimulation, and extremes of temperature. Space for crib babies should insure at least three feet between cribs.

If a kitchenette is not an integral part of the equipment, a bottle warmer and storage space for such food as the parents may bring should be provided.

Their Rooms

Where the number of babies, toddlers, and two-year-olds exceeds ten to twelve pupils for each of these age groupings, separate rooms should be provided. Some leaders suggest that not more than eight toddlers should be placed in one room. Where the pupil load per room does not warrant it, or separate rooms are not available for each of these groups, the space may be divided for better control and protection of the pupils by resorting to the use of portable screens or movable storage cabinets.

Rooms assigned to these children should be large, cheerful but not gaudy, well lighted, ventilated and heated, and hospital clean. For sanitary reasons, visitors should not be allowed in these rooms. A separate reception area should, wherever possible, be arranged for, where these children can be received and returned to those bringing them to the church school. If possible, a small additional room adjoining the classroom should be provided so that a child who is ill or upset can be withdrawn from other children and given special care by teacher or parents.

Particular attention will need to be given to the floor surfaces. These areas should be warm, clean, and covered with plastic, rubber, or asphalt tile. A well finished hardwood floor, while more difficult to maintain, is also acceptable but not recommended. Small washable rugs should be available to protect the children and to make them comfortable while resting or working or playing on the floor surface, where they spend a great deal of their time.

Their Equipment

Provision should be made for cribs, play pens, and such toys and other materials as will permit their being readily cleaned and sterilized before each use.

Storage space, preferably movable cabinets rather than walk-in closets, will be required for bed linen, clothing, and toys. Large blocks, pull toys, sterilized rubber dolls, beds, unbreakable dishes, and wooden animals are most useful. Be sure to omit small objects which can be swallowed, which have sharp or injurious surfaces, or have been treated with injurious dyes or paints.

Nursery III (the three-year-olds)

Adventuring as they are, from the shelter of home-life to the more complex experiences of the outside world, these young children need to be given a sense of security, but not overprotection, a sense of being loved and wanted, an opportunity to live, work, and play with other children of their own age under happy conditions. Most of all, they should be afforded a growing awareness of God in terms and experiences which are meaningful to them at their particular stage of development. Such experiences should meet their needs as growing persons, result in felt satisfactions, and issue in a desire to continue in and to repeat what to them have been joyous undertakings.

Their spiritual growth cannot be disassociated from their emotional, social, and physical environment and well-being. They live and learn through a great variety of experiences. Growth during this period is rapid. Impressions and attitudes engendered at this period are lasting.

Children of this age are constantly on the move. Even a trained athlete who attempts for a day to imitate their every movement, will find himself exhausted physically at the end of the day. Play is a means of their growth, and is an integral, a necessary, and a major part of the young child's daily existence. To fail him here is to divorce our teaching efforts from most of his needs and life.

The attention span at this age is very limited. There is need for a variety of toys and objects to implement active minds which move rapidly from one object to another. Children of this age tire readily from their ceaseless activity. Provision should be made for brief rest periods, even during the short school sessions. This entails washable resting mats or carpets on which they can recline, and good ventilation free from drafts and extremes of temperature.

Space and yet more space, is an essential. The younger the child, the more space is required. Children of this age should not be crowded or cramped in their movements or irritated by unnecessary restrictions imposed by limited floor space, or inadequate teaching procedures. Adequate space will permit the child's participation in a variety of purposeful activities so he may happily "grow in wisdom, in stature, and in favor with God and man."

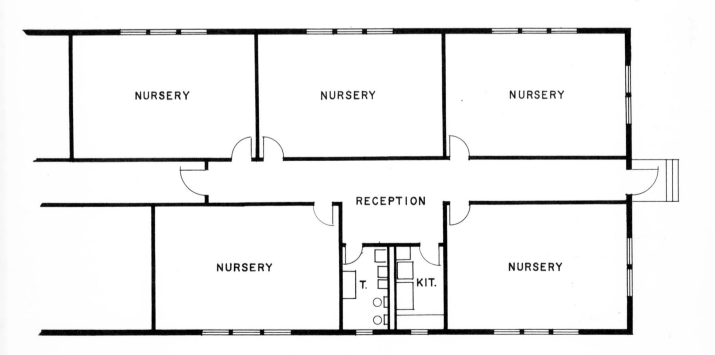

Nursery Arrangement for a Large Church

Note the reception area where the children are brought by the parents. This department is also equipped with toilet facilities and a kitchenette where food can be kept and prepared as needed.

Number of Pupils per Room

Up to fifteen children in one group is considered good. This permits freedom of movement and personal relationships with the leaders. Overcrowding is often a frightening experience for the very small child. He needs individual attention and affection.

Fifteen to eighteen pupils per room is considered fair. While a group of this size permits some individual guidance, if there is a sufficient number of teachers or assistant leaders, the room is liable to be crowded, and the teaching will suffer thereby.

More than eighteen pupils in a room is considered poor. Pupils are crowded, overstimulated, and confused by contacts with too many persons and in too limited an area.

Space Requirements

Space should permit all activities which are planned for a given age group of children to occur in their one room and the adjacent out-of-doors space assigned to them.

While government standards call for forty square feet per pupil in a weekday nursery, for church school purposes the following standards are recommended:

Thirty to thirty-five square feet per pupil is rated good. This permits space for moving about freely among the interest centers within the room, so necessary for the effective teaching of young children.

Twenty-five to thirty square feet per pupil is rated fair. While providing for interest centers and the normal teaching needed for this age group, crowding and irritation of pupils are liable to occur.

Under twenty-five square feet per pupil is rated poor. Such limited space does not permit the free movement of the children, nor provide room enough for interest centers. Overcrowding leads to overstimulation and ineffective teaching.

Direct entrance to the section of the building assigned to pre-school children is recommended. Accessibility to out-of-doors space and a play yard is also recommended.

A room for group activities other than those mentioned above is not needed for children under three years of age.

No room used by pre-school children should be smaller than 15 feet by 20 feet, even if this requires a combination of two age groups. As previously recommended, movable screens or movable shelves can be used to divide the space and to separate the groups where necessary.

Rooms should be rectangular in shape with the long dimension, if at all possible, on the outside wall to permit the largest possible window areas. One wall in each room should be unbroken by doors, windows, and offsets.

Nursery and kindergarten rooms preferably should be used exclusively by pre-school children, for the reason that their equipment does not permit ready adjustment to adult usage.

It is advisable to have the rooms assigned to these children accessible to parents' rooms and adjacent to the primary department into which they will soon be graduating.

It is important that children's rooms be well lighted with natural light for daytime use by means of ample window space. These windows, as previously indicated, should be low enough so the children can see out-of-doors, providing the view is pleasing.

Wherever possible, separate toilet facilities immediately accessible from children's classrooms should be installed, and equipped with juvenile-sized equipment.

Sinks in classrooms are desirable, and should be equipped with counter space, and installations should be at child height.

Floor surfaces are in need of the same special attention as set forth in previous recommendations for Nurseries I and II.

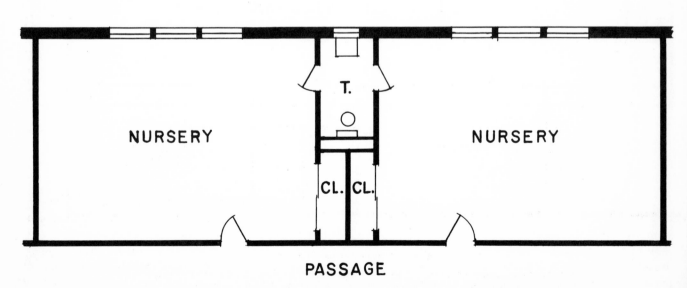

Floor Plan for a Two Room Nursery with a Toilet and Closet Space Serving Both Rooms

Equipment

While it is not necessary to provide a chair for each child in attendance, such chairs as are provided should be 8 inches to 10 inches in height from the floor to the top of the seat. If only one height is used, the 8-inch size is preferred.

Tables should be 10 inches higher than the chair seat. If space is limited, tables may be omitted. Table tops should measure approximately 24 inches by ·36 inches or 28 inches by 42 inches. A low book table will be found useful and a piano, while not essential, can readily be used to advantage.

A Bible, suitable pictures within the interest range of children of this age, housekeeping toys, a songbook or a collection of songs suitable for children of this age, large blocks (2″ x 4″ x 8″ and 2″ x 4″ x 12″), floor toys such as cars, trucks, trains and boats, balls, books, are some of the basic requirements in the way of equipment.

If space permits, the following items may be added later: easels for painting, together with paper and paints, sets of steps and large hollow blocks, and additional housekeeping toys such as brooms, an ironing board, a small iron, clothesline, doll carriage sized for children of this age, and large puzzles.

Kindergartens I and II (four- and five-year olds)

Children of this age have many of the characteristics of the three-year-olds. They are, however, more mature, and show more advanced skills and aptitudes, and need extra equipment to further their development.

The Number of Pupils per Room

The size of the group is slightly increased over that of the three-year-olds. The same reasons for the number of pupils per room govern here as for the younger pupils. Up to twenty pupils of this age in a group is rated good; twenty to twenty-five pupils, fair; and over twenty-five pupils, poor.

Space Requirements

The same general standards and for the same general reasons recommended for the three-year-olds obtain for the four- and five-year-old children, namely:

Thirty to thirty-five square feet per pupil is rated *good;*

Twenty-five to thirty square feet per pupil, *fair;*

Less than twenty-five square feet per pupil, *poor.*

No room for children four and five years old, inclusive, should be smaller than 15 by 20 square feet, even

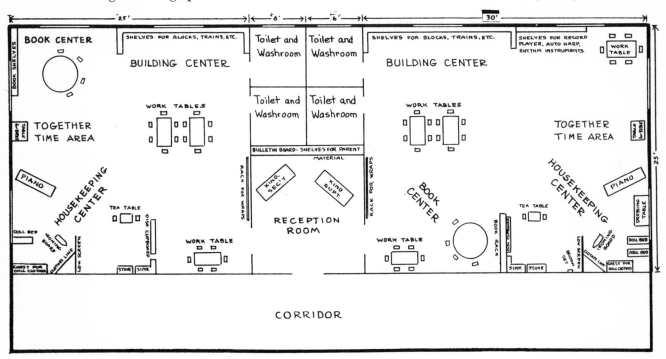

A Plan for a Complete Kindergarten Department

When it is possible to provide two rooms, one for the fours and one for the fives, together with a common reception room, this is a practical plan and is highly recommended. Each room is adequate for twenty kindergarten children.

Low open shelving for the storage of these items and other materials should also be included in the equipment.

A picture rail placed at eye level of the children, an offering container, a waste basket, growing plants, an aquarium or other nature materials, will add to the interest and enjoyment of the children.

if such makes necessary the temporary combination of two age groups until such time as the church can provide the rooms recommended.

As previously recommended, rooms should generally be rectangular in shape with the proportion of 3 feet to 4 feet or 4 feet to 5 feet in width to that of length, and free from pillars and posts and jutting walls. The long dimension of each room should, wherever possible, be on the outside wall to permit plenty of window area. One wall of each room should be unbroken by doors or windows.

The church with limited opportunity for growth and only ten to fifteen children in the pre-school group, can make one room of adequate size serve the total group, provided the three-year-olds are given a separate space within the room to function separately. Churches with a growth expectancy, will need to provide separate rooms at the outset.

Furnishings and Equipment

Chairs for this age group should be from 10 inches to 12 inches in height. If only one height is used, the 10-inch size is preferred. Tables should be 10 inches higher than the chair seat. Table tops should measure 24 inches by 36 inches or 28 inches by 42 inches except where tables are used for books and work activities. These should measure 24 inches by 42 inches or 28 inches by 48 inches. Such tables are not essential if floor space is limited. Where possible, a piano should be included in the equipment.

A Bible and suitable pictures are needed for this age group. Toys are suggested and include large blocks measuring 2 inches by 4 inches by 8 inches and 2 inches by 4 inches by 12 inches. Floor toys for dramatic plays, books, housekeeping toys, paper, scissors, large crayons, a songbook or collection of songs recommended for this group, should also be provided.

Where space permits, easels for painting, paper, and paints, large hollow blocks, large puzzles, sets of wooden animals and people for block play, small aprons, nurses' caps, pocketbooks, ties, and items for dramatic play and in the housekeeping center, will be found most valuable.

A place for wraps for both children and teachers, preferably in a movable cabinet, are required.

As in other children's rooms, low shelves for toys, a place for teachers' supplies, a picture rail at the child's eye level, an offering container, a waste basket, growing plants, an aquarium and other nature materials, together with a display or tack strip space, will be needed.

It is important that children's classrooms should not be cluttered with bulky furniture, bric-a-brac, old pews and pianos which needlessly occupy valuable floor space to no good purpose.

Each item of equipment and furnishing should be selected with particular care to insure that it is needed and that it furthers the learning process. Tables and chairs should be well constructed of good wood, of proper height, and designed for proper posture. Children should be comfortably seated if we are to expect their interest and attention. Pictures need special attention as to quality and subject matter, and should be hung at the eye level of the children.

Convenience and Comfort

Washbasins for children in Kindergartens I and II should be twenty-four inches from the floor, and toilet facilities ten inches from the floor. Use wooden steps where adult fixtures have been installed and must be used for children of this age.

Coat storage at child height with a shelf above for caps and another space below for overshoes, should be placed within the room used by these smaller children. (See Summary at the end of this chapter.)

Interest, Beauty, and Wonder

Kindergarten children grow spiritually in an environment which carries intimations of God. Interest centers arranged for each teaching situation afford firsthand pleasurable encounters with beauty, books, nature, housekeeping, and block building.

A lovely picture, a Bible and an attractive offering basket on a low table with a pretty cover, combine to present a beauty center about which the leader and teacher gather for a Bible story, a song, or a period of appreciation, as circumstances dictate.

A number of interest centers will stimulate attention, moments of worship, and conversation between teacher and child. A low table with a lovely picture and an offering basket or some beautiful object dear to the child, a rack of books attractively arranged, a housekeeping center equipped with suitable implements, a nature center with things a child can bring or enjoy, a quiet corner where children can sit quietly to enjoy books and puzzles are most useful. Furniture should be kept at a minimum where floor space is limited. Where it is not possible to have the ideal room, improve and make the most of what you have while you crusade for better facilities and equipment.

Spontaneous worship arising under guidance out of situations meaningful to the child will make God more real than a socalled, "worship period," imposed upon him as a routine procedure.

Play

Again, we emphasize the importance of providing for the play experiences for these children. These experiences provide a natural way of learning and growing. It is God's plan for the children's normal development. It is the child's way of initiating and entering into the life of adults whom he admires and desires to imitate.

Where space within the building or an adjacent play yard permits, provide such play equipment as slides, walking boards, large lightweight cylinders, boxes, rubber balls, wagons, a jungle gym, doll houses, etc.

Lest We Forget

Rooms assigned to preschool children should be on the sunny side of the building, on the first floor, and above ground level for easy access to the building for them and their parents. Stairways present a safety hazard for both parents with children in arms and for the children. Long dark corridors and rooms with very high ceilings or lacking in outside window exposure have an unhappy effect on the very young children. Direct access to that part of the building used by these children is preferred inasmuch as it protects them from the confusion and noise of the central corridors. It also permits ready exit for out-of-doors activity in play areas. It is important that the first impressions be those of security, a homelike atmosphere, and friendliness.

The time is passing when children are given dark basement rooms or relegated to—just any kind of space.

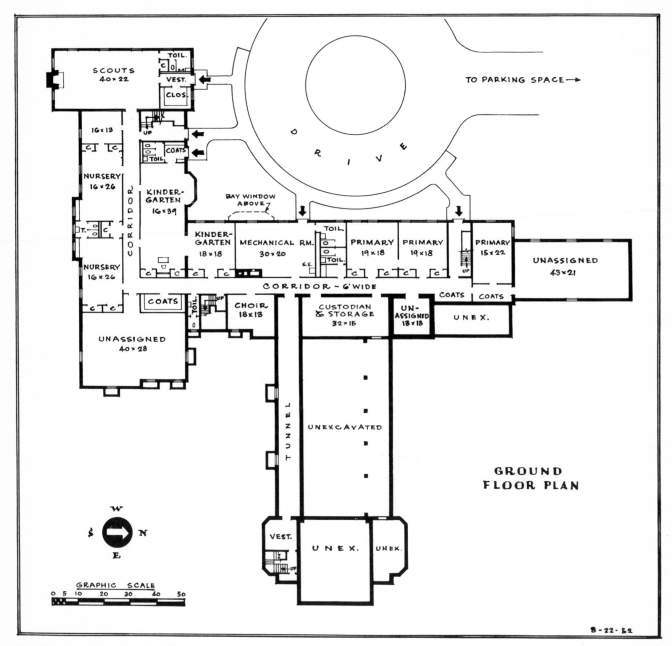

First floor rooms for preschool children provide easy access to out-of-doors.

Charles F. Cellarius, architect

Age Group	Maximum Children Per Room	Floor Space Per Child	Toilets, Sinks, Drinking Fountains	Wraps	Cabinets
Nursery I Babies and Toddlers Age birth to 2	8-10 (Cribs at 3'0" intervals)	35 square feet—good; 30 square feet—fair; under 25 square feet—poor. Separate room for babies and toddlers.	Toilets and wash-basins within pre-school room area preferred. Otherwise, observe strictest sanitation facilities for storing and warming food.	Rod hangers **in the room.** (Preferably in storage cabinet with shelf above and below.) 30 inches above floor. Full length for teachers. Hooks are hazardous. Not recommended.	Movable, ample for supplies.
Nursery II Age 2.	8—Good 10—Fair 12—Poor	35 square feet—good; 30 square feet—fair; under 25 square feet—poor. (Warm, clean floors for children to sit on. All pre-schoolers.)	Adjoining room with junior fixtures or wooden step if adult fixtures used. Toilets 10 inches; basins 24 inches above floor.	Rod hangers **in the room.** (Preferably in storage cabinet with shelf above and below.) 30 inches above floor. Full length for teachers. Hooks are hazardous. Not recommended.	Movable, ample for supplies needed. Low open shelves for toys.
Nursery III Age 3	Up to 15—Good 15-18—Fair Over 18—Poor	35 square feet—good; 30 square feet—fair; under 25 square feet—poor.	Adjoining room with junior fixtures or wooden step if adult fixtures used. Toilets 10 inches; basins 24 inches above floor.	Rod hangers **in the room.** (Preferably in storage cabinet with shelf above and below.) 36 inches above floor. Full length for teachers. Hooks are hazardous. Not recommended.	Movable, ample for supplies needed. Low open shelves for toys. Space for filing pictures and materials used in room. Open shelves for toys.
Kindergarten I, II Ages 4 & 5	Up to 20—Good 20-25—Fair Over 25—Poor	35 square feet—good; 30 square feet—fair; under 25 square feet—poor.		Rod hangers **in the room.** (Preferably in storage cabinet with shelf above and below.) 42 inches above floor. Full length for teachers. Hooks are hazardous. Not recommended.	Movable, ample for supplies needed. Low open shelves for toys. Space for filing pictures and materials used in room. Open shelves for toys.

Rooms on first floor and above grade level.

[1] Presbyterian Church in the U.S.A.

Display Space	Furniture	Other Materials[2]
Grooved picture rail 14″ above floor. Tack board extending from 14″ to 38″ above the floor.	Cribs—preferably bassinets on metal frames with rubber tires. Play pens, bed linen, plastic mats for play pens.	
Grooved picture rail 17″ above the floor. Tack board extending 17″ to 43″ above the floor.	Chairs 6 inches from floor. Not needed for every child. Tables, height 16 inches—small. Tops 18 inches by 24 inches. A book table—not essential if space limited.	Large blocks (2″ x 4″ x 8″ and 2″ x 4″ x 12″); floor toys (peg wagon, wooden, train, cars); books, pictures; a Bible; cuddly toys (stuffed animals, rag dolls); housekeeping toys (doll, doll bed, tea table and dishes); ball; picture rail; offering container; wastebasket; growing plants or other nature materials; a songbook, or collection of songs, recommended in the literature for use by the leaders. Add later (where space permits) walking board; more housekeeping equipment (pans, telephone, small rocking chair); push-and-pull toys; small wagon, resting mats; washable rug or rugs for floor.
Grooved picture rail 20″ above the floor. Tack board extending from 20″ to 48″ above floor.	Chairs 8 inches from floor. A few 6 inches. Tables, height 18 inches. Tops 24″ x 36″ or 28″ x 42″. Teacher's table 18″ x 24″. Piano—not essential, but desirable.	Large blocks (2″ x 4″ x 8″ and 2″ x 4″ x 12″); floor toys (cars, trucks, train, boat); ball; books; a Bible; pictures; housekeeping toys; a songbook, or collection of songs, recommended in the literature for use by the leaders; offering container; wastebasket; growing plants or other nature materials. Add later (where space permits) easels for painting; paint; set of steps; large hollow blocks; more housekeeping toys (broom, ironing board, iron, clothesline, doll carriage—large enough to come to waist of child); large puzzles, sets of wooden animals and people for block play; low bench or stools near place for wraps.
Grooved picture rail 24″ above floor. Tack board extending from 24″ to 54″ above floor.	Chairs 10 inches from floor. Tables, height 20 inches. Tops 24″ x 42″ or 28″ x 48″. Piano desirable.	Large blocks (2″ x 4″ x 8″ and 2″ x 4″ x 12″); floor toys for dramatic play; books; a Bible; pictures; housekeeping toys; paper; scissors; large crayons; a songbook or collection of songs, recommended in the literature for use by the teachers; offering container; wastebasket; growing plants or other nature materials; display or tackstrip space. Add later (where space permits) easels for painting; paint; large hollow blocks; large puzzles; sets of wooden animals and people for block play; small aprons, nurses' caps, pocketbooks, ties, for dramatic play in housekeeping center.

[2] Margie McCarty, *The Church Plans for Children* (Methodist Publishing House, 1953)

Rooms Needed in Relation to Program and to Size of Church School

Preschool Children[3]

	Church School 1-99	Church School 100-299	Church School 300-499	Church School 500-899	Church School 900 and up
Nursery I Infants & toddlers under 18 mos.	Omit—unless suitable separate space is available.	Omit—unless suitable separate space is available.	Possible here to provide one room for toddlers. If there is a need consider separate room, with cribs and play pens, etc., for those under 18 mos.	Separate crib and play pen room.	Similar to larger church schools,
Nursery II Ages 1½ & 2				Separate room for toddlers.	
Nursery III Age 3	May be necessary to house several 3-year-olds in same room as kindergarten. Try to keep separate parts of the room with one helper.	**Enrollment 8-18** One room that may be kept for just the three year old group. If the church sponsors a week-day nursery school this room and kindergarten room may be used. Have rooms near each other.	**Enrollment 20-30** Two rooms. These may be used during the week by parent groups etc., particularly if a folding partition separates them.	**Enrollment 32-54** Two rooms to be used by 3-year-olds only, or one room used for each of two or three sessions.	but these usually may operate in two sessions,
Kindergarten I, II Ages 4 & 5	**Enrollment up to 12** Separate room. Do not encourage attendance of 3-year-olds at expense of the 4 & 5 year olds.	**Enrollment 16-36** One room that may be used both during the church school hour and the church hour. Limit use by others.	**Enrollment 40-60** Two rooms—one for 4-year-olds and one for 5-year-olds. Again helpful to have rooms adjoining for possible use by adults.	**Enrollment 64-108** Four rooms—two for 4-year-olds and two for 5-year-olds, or two rooms (one for each age) used for two or three sessions.	or three sessions and so have more adequate space for each age group.

[3] Presbyterian Church in the U.S.A.

CHAPTER 9

Meeting the Needs of the Elementary School Children⸺⸺⸺⸺⸺⸺⸺⸺⸺⸺⸺

Who Are They?

These are the children who are now attending public school. We think of them as primaries, grades I to III inclusive (ages 6, 7, and 8 years), and the juniors, grades IV to VI inclusive (ages 9, 10, and 11). They are children with specific human needs, spiritual and otherwise. The wise leader will acquaint himself with these specific needs, order his teaching, determine his building plans, and select his equipment in the light of them.

The Primaries (Ages 6, 7, and 8 Years)

These children, while characterized by continuous activity and seemingly boundless energy, tire easily. A six-year-old, particularly, has great difficulty in sitting still. They are eager to learn, interested in life and things about them, have a growing aptitude for learning to read, and enjoy group activity. They enjoy imaginative dramatic play, have a instinctive desire to collect anything and everything, and are sensitive to the approval or disapproval of their companions and adults. While they, apparently, lack a sense of time or an understanding of history, they do have a widening interest in the world around and in far-off places. Their experiences with other children in public school, their growing ability to read, and to play and work together makes them an interesting group. How we handle them is very important.

How Do They Learn?

Children learn best and most meaningfully by living, playing, worshiping, and working together under skilled direction in fittingly sized groups of their own age span. A variety of purposeful activities and experiences encompassed by a religious faith is required to meet their needs on many levels.

The following are some of the many ways of helping children to become increasingly Christian in their everyday living for which ample space and suitable equipment should be provided:

Dramatization, hymn study, music appreciation, nonprojected visual materials, creative visual materials (such as models), interviews, research in the Bible and other sources, interest groups and centers, worship, directed study, outside assignments, purposive play, use of the Bible and hymnals, appreciation of poetry, working in smaller groups, engaging in discussions, arranging and studying curios and exhibits.

Many of the older children will do creative writing. They will also enjoy and participate in choral speaking and in sharing projects. Stories are an unending source of interest to children of this age.

Grouping

Boys and girls should be grouped together naturally as at home, in the public schools, and in the community. Each has a good effect upon the other. It is important to have these children work in a group which is large enough to permit them to work, plan, study and live together in terms within their interest and aptitudes. It is equally important that the group should not be too large and unwieldy and thereby deprive the children of the personal attention and supervision which they need. If the group covers too wide an age span, it will be difficult to find a common interest by means of which the whole group can be held together and work as a team.

It will thus be recognized that the grouping of children of this age will inevitably vary with the average attendance figures of differing churches. Twenty to twenty-five pupils per room under the direction of a leader and assistants is the recommended way of handling the pupil-teaching methods at this age level. Under this arrangement, all activities are carried out within the room.

The following schedule is offered by way of suggestion to enable churches to arrange the groupings in keeping with their attendance figures:

Up to twenty-five primary-junior children combined —one room, twenty to thirty square feet per child.

Up to twenty-five primary children—one room, twenty to thirty square feet per child.

Up to twenty-five junior children—one room, twenty to thirty square feet per child.

Up to forty-five primary children—three rooms, one larger than the other two, where they may meet sometimes as a total group.

Up to forty-five junior children—three rooms, one larger than the other two, where they may meet as a total group at times.

Where a combination of grades is necesary to maintain a good working group, the following arrangement is suggested:

Up to twenty-five first and second grade pupils combined—one room, twenty to thirty square feet per pupil.

Up to twenty-five third and fourth grade pupils combined—one room, twenty to thirty square feet per pupil.

Up to twenty-five fifth and sixth grade pupils combined—one room, twenty to thirty square feet per pupil.

Where there are enough children in each of the grades to divide the group of up to twenty-five in attendance, one room with twenty to thirty square feet per child should be provided for each grade.

Where the number of pupils exceeds twenty-five, other additional rooms should be provided.

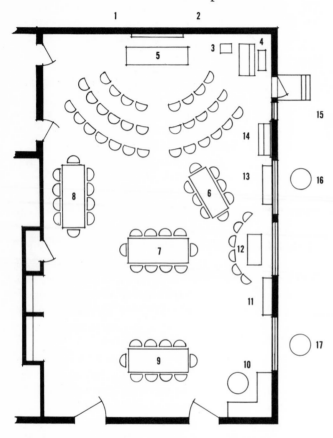

1. Picture rail with groove (See illustration p. 41)
2. Retractible screen for picture projection
3. Record player with record storage beneath
4. Piano
5. Low living room type of table which can be used as a part of an informal worship center
6, 7, 8, and 9, work tables with chairs. (See tabulated equipment details at end of chapter)
10. Happy corner—note one small round table
11. Bookcase
12. Show and tell table
13. Planting board with flowers growing
14. Nature center
15. Church lawn accessible directly from classroom
16. Bird bath
17. Feeding station

Where there are three rooms for the primary department or the junior department it will be possible, by careful planning, to have two of the three rooms of the areas recommended above, and one of the rooms slightly larger. This will permit the assembling of the whole department on the few occasions when it is necessary to bring them together. It should be stated, however, that this is only possible when the total department does not exceed forty-five in average attendance.

Space is not sufficient in itself. The place where we seek to afford our children an awareness of God should be so arranged and appointed as to predispose the child to like and accept wholeheartedly this evidence of the Christian way of life. The needs of the children should dictate the plans and govern the pocketbook of the church constituency.

Someone has aptly said, "We shape our buildings and afterwards our buildings shape us." Clergymen, teachers, and architects, therefore, would be well advised to read the excellent material available describing intimately the psychology of childhood and the effect of environment.

Large expenditures of funds are not always necessary to produce the required effect. An intimate knowledge of the needs, skills, good taste, and the use of the right proportions, color, light, and fabrics all make the difference, and give character and beauty to a room which might otherwise be very cold and boxlike in appearance.

We emphasize again the importance of keeping children out of basements. Interior rooms without any outside light, and dingy, poorly ventilated and depressing surroundings, should be avoided. Clear glass windows with simple treatment providing a pleasant outdoor view make the wide outside an intimate adjunct to the learning experience of children. This delivers them from the sense of being imprisoned and too closely confined.

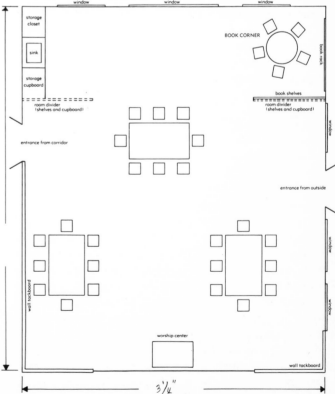

A suggested room for either twenty-five Primary or Junior children with three teachers—one of whom is a leading teacher.

38

Room Space and Equipment

From what has previously been stated, it is evident that large rooms for every twenty to twenty-five primary children are essential. Each room should be self-contained and adaptable to all activities. Twenty to thirty square feet of floor space per child is recommended, with the understanding that an additional 10 per cent of the total floor space should be provided for cabinet storage space. Twenty-five to thirty square feet per pupil is rated good; twenty to twenty-five square feet fair; below twenty square feet, poor.

It is becoming increasingly necessary that children's rooms be designed for flexibility in use to meet the needs of the changing procedures of the church.

As has already been suggested, a church building should be so designed that partitions dividing classroom areas are nonbearing, and can be removed or restored without serious cost or mutilation of the structure as a whole. Rooms should also be designed for multiple use, both for Sunday and weekday undertakings. This will result in serving more people and in realizing a greater return on the money invested. If multiple sessions are to be held, it will be necessary to provide a great deal more storage space than has hitherto characterized church school buildings. Needless to say, adequate leadership with assistants who understand the new teaching procedures and can work together as a team, will make the best use of the recommended space and equipment.

It is not necessary here to repeat in detail references already made to the importance of the right use of light and color in giving a pleasing character to the room in which these children live and work. Chapters II and VI, in which we deal with environment and color, give many helpful suggestions in this connection.

Built-in, formally arranged worship centers or children's chapels are not recommended for children of primary age. This tends to freeze room-use, and make worship a mockery. Simple, informal worship is a far better preparation to worship than formalized centers or chapels could ever be. A piano, properly tuned, should be provided, if at all possible.

Inasmuch as children of this age work with materials which stain their hands, it is advisable to provide a sink with running water, and sink shelves installed at the proper height for this age group within the classroom or immediately accessible thereto. If the building funds permit, it is well to have toilet facilities installed, preferably in a space between the classrooms used by pupils of the same general age level. If such an ideal arrangement is not possible, the toilet rooms should be on the same floor and readily accessible.

Previous reference has been made concerning the floor surfaces which are necessary for the health, comfort, and convenience of these children.

Children of this age can make use of bulletin and chalk boards. These boards should be constructed so they can be hung on the walls and moved from place to place when necessary. Again, we emphasize the value of movable storage cabinets which will take care of books, posters, globes, objects of interest used by the children, and finished work, paper, pencils, drawing equipment, etc. These cabinets can also be used to divide the floor space for the different work or interest groups as the program of the day may require. These low barriers do not obstruct the view of the pupils, nor separate and estrange them from the group as a whole. They do, however, provide some control and separation of function and, while maintaining the sense of the group working together as a whole, they afford a mild means of furthering the good discipline of the room.

It is recommended that storage space be provided in cabinets which can be moved from room to room, if reassignment of space to other age groups is necessary. These cabinets will need to be carefully designed for the particular requirements of this age group. Rods and hooks for children's clothing should be

pictures and handiwork can be exhibited, will add to the interest and efficiency of the working space.

In selecting materials, it is recommended that materials be carefully selected for their excellence and that, if the budget is limited, the basic items be selected first. The preparation of a fully detailed list will serve as a goal to be reached as funds become available. In view of the great amount of material available, churches should be warned against buying too many items of inferior quality or items very remotely related to the curriculum of the church school.

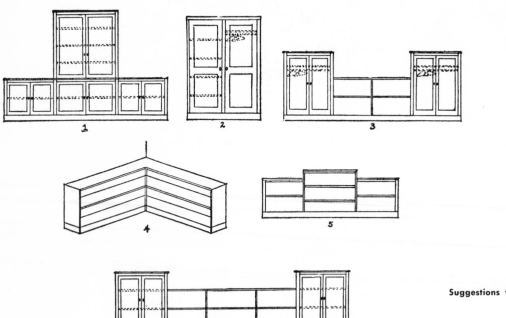

1. Closed cabinet space for children and teachers
2. Cabinet for teachers' supplies and teachers' wraps
3. Open shelves with place for children's wraps at either end
4. Corner shelves
5. Open shelves
6. Open shelves with closed space for teachers' supplies at either end

Suggestions for Facilities

placed at the proper height, and preferably in the adjacent corridor, where they are readily accessible to the pupils.

Chairs should be 12 inches to 14 inches from floor to the top of the seat. If only one height is used, the 14-inch height is preferred. Tables should be 10 inches higher than the chair seat. Table tops should be approximately 30 inches by 48 inches or 30 inches by 54 inches. A smaller table for a beauty or a worship center is suggested. Open shelves for storage materials which are thereby made accessible to the children, and a cabinet for teachers' supplies, need to be included in the general equipment.

Books and supplementary materials recommended in the teaching manuals and by denominational educational leaders for this age group, should be included in the equipment for the leaders' use. Bibles, papers, pencils, crayons, paste, scissors, songbooks for both the pianist and teacher, pictures, books chosen according to the unit being studied, simple reference books, and song charts, are some of the basic requirements.

Display and tack-strip space at the eye level of the children, growing plants and other nature materials, wastepaper basket, picture rail, preferably grooved and about 3 inches in width from which

Juniors (Ages 9, 10, 11—Grades 4, 5, and 6)

Children of this age show some advance over their younger friends of the primary department in alertness, eagerness for information, and in their growing capacity to think and reason. Eye co-ordination is good, hands are ready for craft and shop activities. These children are capable of more prolonged attention. Their interest and attention span is increased over that of younger children, and they now have an ability to plan ahead. They are interested in the ideas of other people, and possess an expanding knowledge and interest in the physical world—laws of nature, stars, earth, and their own physical makeup. They are studying history in the public schools, and are interested in people who have done great and brave deeds. They are now reading to learn instead of learning to read. Individual differences are now distinct and clear, and will need to be skillfully met. Juniors like teamwork, group activities, and clubs, but are likely to resent too much adult supervision of activities.

Differences in the aptitudes and interests of girls and boys become more evident, and need to be handled with sympathetic understanding. At this stage there is usually a developing interest in the opposite sex which sometimes leads to teasing between boys and girls.

Play interests sometimes become sharply different. Girls of this age are likely to grow faster than boys and, as a consequence, the leader and her assistants will need to be constantly on the alert to make the adjustments and to keep the group appreciative of their individual members and still related to the overall procedures of the department.

Juniors have a strong sense of right and wrong, and are susceptible to the good opinion and the standards of conduct of adults. They also manifest an aptitude for assuming responsibility and a growing dependability.

Grouping

Children of junior age follow approximately the same patterns as we have previously recommended in this chapter for primaries and primary-junior combinations, namely, that large rooms for every 20 to 25 junior age children are essential. Each room should be self-contained and adaptable to all activities. Twenty to thirty square feet of floor space per child is recommended, with the understanding that an additional 10 per cent of the total floor space should be provided for cabinet storage space. Twenty-five to thirty square feet per pupil is rated good; twenty to twenty-five square feet fair; below twenty square feet, poor.

Space and Equipment

Generally speaking, the same general standards both for the appointments of the room and its equipment hold for the juniors as for the primaries. There will be a few exceptions, inasmuch as these children are older, have more skill, and different interests. Physically they are larger, and the furnishings will need to be selected accordingly.

Chair heights should be 15 inches and 17 inches from floor to the top of the seat. If only one height is used, the 16-inch height is preferred. Tables should be 10 inches higher than the chair seats. Tops should measure approximately 30 inches by 48 inches or 30 inches by 54 inches. Smaller tables for worship centers, for beauty centers, and other special uses, are recommended. A piano, shelves for materials used by the children, and cabinets for teachers' supplies, should be designed in keeping with the requirements of this age group and the materials they use.

CROSS SECTION
GROOVED PICTURE RAIL

Display and tack strips, storage of wraps, and other terials suggested as the equipment for the primary department, should also be installed in the junior rooms.

The recommended literature for this age group, a departmental Bible, and a smaller Bible for each child, songbooks so each child may have one, pictures graded to the interest and understanding of the children, books carefully chosen according to the unit being studied and in keeping with the capacities of the child; paper, pencils, crayons, paste, scissors, etc. are basic requirements.

Later, it may be found wise to include a Bible dictionary, a Bible atlas, maps, a globe, reference books, copies of different translations of the Bible, and an English dictionary.

Inasmuch as audio-visual materials will be a part of the teaching equipment of this age group, attention is directed to Chapter XII, where detailed suggestions as to their use are to be found.

Here again, we counsel against too hasty a selection of too many things. Be sure to confer with accredited leaders, and selected materials which can be immediately used and of a quality which meets with the approval of the best minds in the field of Christian education.

Rooms Needed by Elementary Children as Related to School Size [2]

	Church School 1–99	Church School 100–299	Church School 300–499	Church School 500–899	Church School 900 and up
Primary Grades 1-2-3	**Enrollment up to 18** One room where age group can meet, but if necessary along with the entire church school session. May be part of large space divided.	**Enrollment 24–54** One room; or one large room and one medium size room for approximately 25. Two grades can use large room for all purposes. One grade can use smaller room for all purposes or unite with the other two grades	**Enrollment 60–90** Three rooms—one for each school grade, to be treated as three separate groups; or may come together occasionally for worship or other purposes.	**Enrollment 96–162** Six rooms—or three if there is a second session. Handle as separate groups.	Have more adequate space for each age group.
Junior Grades 4-5-6	**Enrollment up to 15** One room or part of room in which juniors may be alone for at least 45 minutes a Sunday. May have to worship some of the time with older groups in the church school.	**Enrollment 20–45** Same as requirements for Primary children.	**Enrollment 50–75** Three rooms, one for each grade; or one large room and one medium size for approximately 30.	**Enrollment 80–135** Same as for Primary.	

[2] Presbyterian Church in the U.S.A.

Summary of Space and Equipment for Elementary School Children

Age Group	Maximum Children Per Room	Floor Space Per Child	Toilets, Basins, Drinking Facilities	Wraps	Cabinets	Display Space	Furniture	Other Materials[3]
Primary Grades 1, 2, 3 Ages 6, 7, 8	Up to 25—Good 25-30—Fair 30-35—Poor (See comment below for assembly) (Preferably on first floor, above grade level)	30 sq.ft.—Good 25 sq.ft.—Fair 20 sq.ft.—Poor	Separate toilets for boys, girls. Readily accessible on same floor. Wash basins 28" from floor. Toilets 14" from floor. Sink with running water and double drain board in room preferred.	Some prefer in room. Use rod hangers 42" to 48" above floor, shelf above.	Ample space carefully planned for pupils' and teachers' supplies, handiwork, picture storage. Open shelves for books.	Grooved picture rail 30" above the floor. Tack board 30" to 62" above the floor. Portable black boards or turn-over charts made for handling and tack boards on one or two sides of room.	Chairs 14" from floor, some 12". Table tops 30" x 48" or 54", 24" high. Small tables for beauty or worship centers. Piano. Record player.	Recommended literature, One or more Bibles, Paper, pencils, crayons, paste, scissors. Songbook for pianist and teacher's use (one recommended in the literature). Pictures, books chosen according to unit being studied; simple reference books. Song charts. Growing plants or other nature materials, waste basket, picture rail, movable blackboard or large sheets of newsprint on an easel may be desired. See Chapter 12 for audio-visuals.
Juniors Grades 4, 5, 6	Up to 25—Good 25-30—Fair 30-35—Poor Up to 45 Pupils, 3 rooms; 1 larger for assembly at times.	20-30 sq.ft.— Good 25 sq.ft.—Fair 20 sq.ft.—Poor	As above except basins 30", toilets 16" from floor.	Some prefer in room, otherwise in recessed corridor storage space. Use rod hangers 48-54 in. above floor, shelf above.	Same as above but provide storage for maps, large objects.	Grooved picture rail 36" above the floor. Tack board 36" to 72" above floor.	Chairs 16" from floor. Table tops 30" x 48" or 54", 26" high. Piano. Small tables for beauty and worship center. Record player.	Recommended literature, a Bible for the department, a Bible for each child, Songbooks for children's use (one recommended in the literature). Pictures, Books chosen according to unit being studied, Paper, pencils, crayons, paste, scissors; Offering container, Waste basket, Growing plants or other nature materials, Picture rail, Movable blackboard or large sheets of newsprint on an easel may be useful. **Add later** Bible dictionary; Bible atlas, maps, a globe, reference books, copies of different translations of the Bible, a dictionary.

[1] Emma Jane Kramer, *Equipment and Arrangement for Children's Groups in the Church* (Board of Education, The Methodist Church, 1946)

[2] Presbyterian Church in the U.S.A.

[3] Margie McCarty, *The Church Plans for Children* (Methodist Publishing House, 1953)

CHAPTER 10

Meeting the Needs of Youth......................................

Youth Today

The youth of today reflect the time and spirit of the age which engulfs them. It is a period of high tension, fearful uncertainty, and political and social upheaval. The traditional landmarks of morality have been obscured by the all too prevalent dereliction on the part of persons holding high places in our national life. The current struggle for success popularly measured by monetary and material standards has relegated the idealism of our Christian faith to a secondary place in the practical concerns of many persons. The prevailing mood is a witch's bitter brew of cynicism and uncertainty. The ensuing traits are found in the irresponsibility, the nervousness, and the abnormal demand for thrills which characterize persons of all ages and which particularly and understandably affect our youth.

From within themselves, youth are subject, as always, to the stresses inherent in their development from childhood to the physical, intellectual maturity of adulthood. Their inherent capacity for idealism needs to be extricated from the prevailing materialism which measures life in terms of being well adjusted, popular, and successful. These young people need the love and companionship of persons of understanding. They need to be confronted with that habitual vision of greatness exemplified in the person of Jesus Christ. They need the best we can provide in leadership and equipment.

In Particular

For purposes of organization and good teaching procedures, we think of youth as being: junior high pupils, ages twelve, thirteen, and fourteen years, grades seven, eight, nine; senior high pupils, ages fifteen, sixteen, seventeen years, grades ten, eleven, twelve; and older youth, ages eighteen to twenty-three years inclusive, or to the time of marriage or the assumption of other adult responsibilities.

It is evident that there is a wide range of needs, interests, aptitudes, and capacities in a group of this age range which we call "youth." Worship, study, discussion, recreation, eating together, dramatics, audio-visuals, service projects, music, hobbies, crafts, scouting, and clubs, are among the activities which make their living, learning, and working together most rewarding. When making plans for its building, the church will need to face up to, and provide as far as possible for all of the activities and interests which

go to make up the total Sunday and weekday youth program. The space and equipment should be ultimately related to the particular requirements of each age level group. In most instances, careful scheduling of events and skillful planning of the building will permit the multiple use of rooms for a variety of undertakings. Storage cabinets within each room and along adjacent corridors designed to store the special equipment or the extra chairs or tables needed will prove invaluable in this connection, and permit a surprisingly varied use of building space. Ten per cent additional floor space added to classrooms for storage cabinets will pay large dividends in their varied and multiple use.

Worship

There is a prevailing trend toward including youth in the worship services of the church on Sunday morning. This tends to eliminate the assembling of this age group by departments during the Sunday church school and to use the Sunday evening fellowships for this purpose.

Provision should be made for both formal and spontaneous worship. A chapel is excellent for formal worship. It can be used on occasion on Sunday morning and, more particularly, for vespers on Sunday evening. Rather than having formal worship centers in youth rooms, it is better to have available storage space for materials from which this age group can make selections and plan their own arrangements.

Audio-Visuals

The greatly increased use of audio-visuals make necessary planning for the use of these materials in all youth rooms. Detailed suggestions on this will be found in Chapter XII.

Recreation

Wholesome recreation is important in youth work. Junior highs, particularly, require opportunities for strenuous physical exercise. Except in rare instances where there is a particular need and funds are available for professional leadership and maintenance, gymnasiums, swimming pools, and bowling alleys are not recommended. Provision for recreation should be made on the church grounds and within the building. The social hall will serve indoors for group games and wholesome fellowship. Basketball and volley ball courts marked off on the parking lot or other available

outdoor space will serve for the greater part of the year in most of our country.

This same group is also interested in discussions. They need a place of their own for limited periods of discussion as an intimate group. They, likewise, along with other youth, should be given opportunity for purposeful activities such as working in the arts and crafts.

Crafts

A room or rooms for purposeful work in the crafts and creative arts can be shared by youth and adults. Such a room need not be as well finished as a classroom. It should be impervious to the "messing" contingent upon its special use, and should have good light, water, and electric outlets adequate for the equipment used. Ample storage cabinets with wide sliding panel doors will be needed to store and protect from week to week the unfinished handicraft projects.

Fellowship

Where possible, youth should have at least one room distinctly theirs which serves as a rendezvous. A browsing table with pertinent books, magazines, a stereopticon viewer, a record player, table games, small light but strong tables, occasional furniture, floor lamps, colorful window draperies, floor coverings, and a generally attractive decor will serve to make such a room attractive, popular, and useful. Where circum-

stances warrant and funds are available, a snack bar might well be included. In some instances, a small pullman kitchen is installed for preparing and serving light refreshments. At least the church kitchen and the fellowship hall can be made available and furnished to meet the needs of young people.

Today, churches are procuring much larger sites than previously. This permits outdoor recreation areas of various kinds including tennis courts, a softball diamond, a place for outdoor vesper services, and a fireplace for fellowship and "cook-outs." Where such facilities are provided, adequate supervision and maintenance are imperative.

Grouping and Classrooms

With the suggestions offered in Chapter V in mind, we now give particular attention to the needs of the grouping and grading of youth. The trend toward larger classes made up of boys and girls applies to all youth groups.

Junior Highs—The number of pupils per classroom should not exceed twenty persons, preferably with two adult leaders. This insures a group large enough for wholesome group experiences and activities and yet small enough to permit individual participation and a close friendly relationship between leaders and pupils. This calls for rooms with floor areas of twenty by fifteen feet = 300 square feet each. Classrooms of this size permit a variety of purposeful activities and a much more fruitful learning experience than the usual small rooms which restrict teaching to lecture, notebook procedures. Separate classrooms for each grade with provision for not less than fifteen square feet per pupil is now recommended. Where the number of pupils exceeds twenty, additional classrooms for each grade will be required for each twenty pupils. Where the attendance for the junior highs does not exceed sixty pupils, one of the three classrooms can be large enough to assemble the three grades, if such occasions occur. For example, sixty pupils can be assembled in a room having some 480 square feet. The recommended classroom for each grade requires twenty by fifteen feet = 300 square feet for each of the three rooms; better still provide one room at 480 square feet, and two rooms at 300 square feet each.

Where churches can successfully operate a multiple session school, the number of classrooms needed for a large youth group can be materially reduced. Care should be exercised under such conditions to insure adequate space for an evening fellowship to permit the age groups to be brought together as a unit.

Senior Highs—Practically all we have said concerning junior highs applies to seniors. The exceptions are found in the recommended pupil load per classroom, namely, twenty-five pupils per room maximum, instead of the lesser number for junior highs. The square footage per pupil per classroom is fifteen square feet. Thus a class of twenty-five seniors requires a room with a floor area of twenty-five by fifteen square feet i.e., 375 square feet. A department of three grades might well plan for one large classroom of approximately 600 square feet, and two smaller rooms of 375 square feet each. This would permit assembling the whole department in the large room, if need for such occurs. Use of a chapel or a fellowship room will serve the few times when it is advisable to assemble the department. (See paragraph on "Worship" above.) Generally speaking, each class can and should function as a unit, carrying on its own Sunday church school program within its own room, with preferably two adult leaders.

We draw attention to the significant rise in the predicted enrollment of junior high and senior high school pupils. This sharp rise will affect the junior highs in 1956 and the seniors in 1959 with consequent demands on building space and equipment.

Youth rooms may be located in practically any part of the church edifice. Where possible, placing them near the fellowship hall and church kitchen permits ready use of these facilities for evening fellowship or informal weekday meetings. Classrooms will serve for committee meetings and project activities. Dividing the large fellowship hall with a folding partition or a row of attractive portable screens, will reduce this room to more intimate proportions, and make it more serviceable for youth purposes.

Basic Equipment

The decor of all youth rooms should reflect good taste. Cheerful but not gaudy color combinations should be in keeping with suggestions offered in Chapter V and Chapter XVI. Soft, cheerful pastel or neutral color tones on walls and woodwork will permit color contrasts and touches of lightness in window draperies, pictures, occasional chairs, flower vases, etc. Rooms so treated can be freshened with new color combinations from time to time without need for a costly redecoration of a whole room.

Some leaders prefer a classroom chair with ample arm rests to accommodate note and reference books. These chairs are expensive, cannot be easily stored or readily moved to other rooms, are restricted to classroom use, curtail their general use, and usurp floor space when not used for formal classroom study. Good sturdy smooth-finished hardwood chairs finished in a neutral stain, affording a correct posture, are preferred. Good quality metal frame folding chairs, if comfortable and conducive to correct posture, have the advantage of ready storage and easy manipulation from place to place when needed.

Sturdy folding work tables with tops approximately the size of a standard card table can be used separately or in combination as needed, and stored readily in a cabinet within the classroom.

A chalkboard—black or green—and a tack board for display purposes, are needed for each classroom. Instead of chalkboards some persons prefer turn-over chart holders equipped with large sheets of white paper. These holders are cleaner, permit turning over pages of written material for back reference, and allow preservation of notes made on previous occasions. They can be easily moved about within the classroom or can be taken to other parts of the church edifice.

Storage cabinets, Bibles, youth hymnbooks, a browsing table with appropriate literature, and a tuned piano are desirable adjuncts for youth classrooms.

Good, even lighting, free from glare, yielding some twenty-five to forty foot candles at table top level, and plenty of conveniently placed electric outlets, are required. (See Chapter XII.) Adequate ventilation free from drafts, and regulated to provide even, standard temperatures, are prime requisites.

Suggested Layout for Youth Rooms

Junior High Assembly and 7th Grade Class	Senior High Assembly and 10th Grade Class	Older Youth Assembly and Class	Older Youth Class	Kitchen for All Youth

Hallway

8th Grade Class	9th Grade Class	11th Grade Class	12th Grade Class	Men's Toilet	Women's Toilet	Library or Classroom

(12-15 sq.ft. per Person in Assembly Rooms)
(15-18 sq.ft. per Person in Classrooms)

Summary of Space and Equipment for Youth[1]

Age Group	Maximum Pupils Per Room	Floor Space Per Pupil	Furniture and Equipment
Junior High I, II, III. Grades 7, 8, 9 Ages 12, 13, 14	20 Pupils, Good 10-15 Pupils— Preferred	15-18 sq.ft.—Good 12-15 sq.ft.—Fair 10-12 sq.ft.—Poor	Lightweight tables without drawers. Space to store extra tables and chairs. Comfortable, sturdy chairs, blackboard or turn-over chart frames with large sheets of paper. Display board, wall maps, youth library, pianos, record player and record storage, recreational equipment and place to store it. Bibles, textbooks, etc.
Senior High and Older Youth Grades 10, 11, 12 Ages 15, 16, 17	25 Pupils Maximum	Same as Above	Equipped for audio-visuals—see Chapter XII. Nearby accessible cloak storage space, toilet facilities. Storage cabinets for pictures, hymnals, materials and supplies. Colorful, attractive furnishings in keeping with decor of building.
Older Youth 18-23 Years			

Provision should be made for recreation, worship, handicraft and hobbies, dramatics, youth choirs and refreshments. See Chapters 10, 11, and 15.

[1] Presbyterian Church in the U.S.A.

Rooms Needed in Relation to Program and to Size of Church School[2]

Youth Division

	Church School 1–99	Church School 100–299	Church School 300–499	Church School 500–899	Church School 900 and up
Junior High	**Enrollment up to 12** Church school class may meet in church pew or in nearby home. For other types of activity, see below.	**Enrollment 12–35** Church school classes may be held in sanctuary if necessary but a meeting space is needed for other program activities.	**Enrollment 35–60** Department Assembly Room, plus two classrooms large enough for classes of 15-20. Assembly room may be used for through-the-week activities.	**Enrollment 60–100** Department Assembly Room with classrooms for groups of 15-20. Assembly room should be available for activities of junior highs throughout the week.	**Enrollment 100–up** Three departments should be provided, one for each grade. Provide each section with an Assembly Room and classrooms.
Senior High	**Enrollment up to 10** Meet in church pews for Church school classes. Junior highs and seniors may meet together for activities other than study and discussion. Ordinarily the church sanctuary, a home nearby, or the fellowship room is available for such use.	**Enrollment 10–30** Same as above. Separate room should be available for program activities.	**Enrollment 24–40** Assembly Room with two classrooms. A third class may meet in the assembly room itself. Such a room also becomes a headquarters for the Youth Fellowship.	**Enrollment 50–90** Department Assembly Room with classrooms for groups of about 20.	**Enrollment 90** Department Assembly and Room with classrooms over for groups of not more than 25.

Older Youth

If older youth are working, they may wish a group of their own or may join with college students. In any event, see suggestions under "Planning for Adults."

If they are attending college away from home, let the college pastor know.

If they are attending college at home, provide for a college-age fellowship. Facilities needed are both those listed in this section and those under "Adult."

For any church to consider:

Where possible the same room should be used for assembly and worship in the church school and also for Sunday evening or through-the-week program. Therefore, it should be suited to a variety of activities and provided with ample storage space for supplies and equipment.

Classrooms should be attractive, efficiently-designed and large enough to allow for ample movement.

Recreation, crafts, hobbies and drama are part of the ongoing program and facilities should be provided for them. A kitchenette is desirable.

For a weekday schedule of activities, room should be easy of access, near a building entrance.

---

[2] Presbyterian Church in the U.S.A.

CHAPTER 11

Meeting the Needs of Adults

Adults—Young and Older

1. The *young adults,* ages twenty-four to thirty-five years approximately. Many of this group are older youth, who have assumed adult responsibilities early in life. There are also the unmarried persons with interests quite different from those of the young married couples who belong to this age classification. This latter group are establishing homes at a phenomenal rate. What we do with and for them and their children is vitally important to the future of the church.

2. The *adults,* ages thirty-six to sixty-four years, approximately. These are the active people of middle age who, together with the young adults furnish most of the leadership of the church and church school.

3. The *older adults,* ages sixty-five years and up. It is estimated that they will soon constitute upwards of 25 per cent of the total population. For the most part, these folk have considerable leisure time and special needs which should receive the special attention of the church.

"The Church," according to the *International Journal of Religious Education,* "has unusual opportunity in providing wholesome friendship and participation in group life through the Sunday school classes, evening fellowship, and many other groups in the church. Although church groups have not always been constructive, they offer great opportunity for individual and for collective growth. Ideally, in such fellowships, each member is accepted, finds friendship, and feels a deep sense of belonging. Each one participates in purposeful activities which enable him to discover his own worth and that of others. The effect of experience in groups of this kind may be 'developmental' (i.e., they may aid in the development of the person), and it may be 'therapeutic' (i.e., having a health effect such as helping to overcome feelings of inadequacy and loneliness)." This statement, which applies to group activities as a whole, has particular pertinence for the adults of the church.

The adult education movement which has gained such wide national recognition, has instituted so many excellent programs both on the national and community levels, invites the co-operation of the Christian Church. This movement has much to offer in the way of techniques which can be adapted by the church in meeting the religious needs of its older citizens.

An appraisal of the program of most churches indicates that the adult program is rather meager or overemphasizes certain aspects of church life, but does not actually meet the needs or draw out the latent possibilities of the adult constituency which make up a large percentage of the church membership. While the majority of this group attend church services, at least occasionally, perhaps belong to a church school class or a young parents' organization, or may even be in a leadership training group, the church has yet to devise a program which goes further and meets and ministers to the needs of this particular segment of its responsibility.

Trends

There is a definite trend away from the large organized classes—teacher centered, sit and listen program—to somewhat smaller group organizations constituted around special interests. In times past, these large adult groups tended to be a church within a church paralleling its program and serving as a substitute for the service of worship which includes the whole church family. Smaller groups, preferably of twenty to twenty-five persons, and not to exceed fifty, provide a more intimate fellowship and a more active participation by those in attendance. In some instances, these smaller groups organized about a special interest or pursuit will reach across all adult age levels and weave them into a common fellowship for discussion, work, study, and mutual enrichment. (See Chapter VII, section on adults.)

Their Interests and Needs

The growing emphasis upon the family program for young parents and their children, lifts up another special interest for inclusion in future building plans. In many churches the classrooms for these parents are placed near those of the preschool and elementary ages groups. Frequently the curriculum for these parents' groups is designed to guide them on the religious nurture of their children and in gaining a religious faith equal to their parental responsibilities. Informal meetings for fellowship where they can gather around some worthy project affords the church its best means for integrating them into the life and work of the church. This is particularly true in these days of mobile population when people are uprooted from their native communities and need to make new friends and church affiliations.

The older adults welcome opportunities for fellowship and for useful service which affords them a sense of belonging, of being wanted and useful, and lessens the feeling of loneliness which often overtakes them in their later years. While they would be the last group to ask for special attention that sets them apart from others, there are certain considerations in planning and equipping a church building which make life much more pleasant and less hazardous for them.

Our church buildings should be built as near ground level as feasible. Approaches should be bridged by slopes, ramps, and steps with risers no higher than five inches. Stairways and steps should be equipped with handrails, care being taken to make these facilities graceful and architecturally fitting. Skid-proof wax now available, should be applied to floor surfaces to prevent painful injury. As a further safety measure, see to it that single steps between floor levels or combinations of two steps are eliminated from your building plans. These are particularly hazardous to older persons.

Proper illumination of all approaches to the building and of passageways and stairways is important. Adequate lighting within rooms used by these people is imperative. Many of them find the harsh light from fluorescent fixtures painful to their eyes. Adequate regulated heat of even temperature along with non-drafty ventilation help to reduce respiratory illnesses. Many of them prefer torrid heat to the chill of air conditioned rooms for their arthritic condition.

We often forget that they find it difficult to stoop and that electric wall plugs should be placed two to three feet above the usual location in the baseboard. Furniture of the right height should be selected. The excessively low furniture now in vogue is a serious handicap to older adults. Recreation and social rooms should include enough comparably hard chairs of standard adult height for the convenience and comfort of these people.

In his article in the *International Journal of Religious Education,* July-August, 1954, titled "Older Adults in the Church Building," from which we have drawn largely for this section, F. Grover Fulkerson reminds us that "a cruel thing that happens to old ladies is that they are run out of the kitchen. . . . With so many old people living in rented rooms or with relatives, all too often perfectly wonderful cooks have no kitchen in which to cook. Hardly anything pleases them more than the opportunity to cook and provide refreshments for their club group. . . . It is tragic if the kitchen of the church is not used as one of the main gathering places for the members who find the church the home they may not have where they are living. A kitchen is not just a place to cook; it is for gossiping, arranging flowers, washing hands and just standing around."[1]

He also reminds us that older persons make more frequent use of toilet facilities than younger folk and for this reason they should not be forced to make long walks or go upstairs in search of rest rooms. These facilities should be obvious and readily available.

Where space and a pertinent program are provided, adults can be brought together on Sunday evenings and weekdays for fellowship, study, work, special events, recreational undertakings and church service activities geared to their interests, abilities, and energies. Many churches have developed programs for creative hobbies such as camera clubs, dramatic groups, and a variety of handicrafts. The products of these fellowships are not only enriching to the participants but provide useful equipment for the church rooms and for publicizing the church's activities. Provision will need to be made for serving teas, providing "snacks," and light lunches, dinners for small groups, and family supper meetings of the church.

Space

Adults will need to be provided with the right kind of space to care for such activities as those referred to. The environment in which adult education takes place is important because it has an influence on the life and attitudes of men and women. Older people, like children and youth, are constantly reacting to their environments, sometimes consciously, often unconsciously. Pleasant surroundings help to create attitudes and experiences that are positive and meaningful, whereas slovenly or unattractive rooms produce impressions that are often negative in character. It is important that adult classrooms be equipped so as to be conducive to the best learning experiences. Every church should be realistic in facing these requirements.

Gymnasiums, large permanent stages, swimming pools, and bowling alleys are not recommended except in very special situations, and then only when professional supervision and maintenance costs can be cared for adequately. Before attempting to install these costly features, the church should make every effort to canvass the communities to see if other community institutions cannot provide for these types of recreation. In many instances, the organization of a community adult education movement will be the way to work out a community program which, while church related, makes use of the facilities which would not otherwise be available to the individual church or group within the church. The Y.M.C.A. and the Y.W.C.A., and even the public school buildings will frequently make their facilities available on a community basis.

Space and equipment for use by adults can be made flexible and adaptable for multiple use by providing adequate storage cabinets and portable equipment. A church living room that serves for women's group meetings on weekdays can be readily adjusted for adult class meetings on Sunday, for Sunday evening or weekday needs for young adults, and for parents' smaller social and study purposes. The same room can serve older adults for their meetings during the week. The room should be of ample size, informally furnished, and have storage space to permit putting away special equipment which is not needed for all of the groups using the room either on Sunday or during weekdays.

Some churches have made a feature of providing a

club room where older adults may come during their leisure time for fellowship, table games, and quiet reading.

Many adults will wish to participate in lighter forms of recreation such as dramatic activities, music groups, and to engage in hobbies and a variety of craft activities. By careful planning, these varied activities can be carried on by multiple use of rooms, if storage space for special equipment is incorporated in the planning.

Activities rooms will require space not less than twelve to twenty square feet per person, and in no case should the room be smaller than twenty by twenty feet. (See Chapter X, section on "Crafts.")

Classrooms

The following recommendations for adult room sace are based on average attendance.

> 1 to 49 adults need 1 to 4 classrooms
> 50 to 99 adults need 2 to 7 classrooms
> 100 to 199 adults need 4 to 10 classrooms
> 200 and up adults need 6 or more classrooms

Regardless of the number of adults or classrooms needed, it should be remembered that the lecture type of teaching, which is not recommended as the sole method to be used, requires eight to ten square feet per person; whereas the activity type of classroom procedure requires twelve to twenty square feet per person. (See section on "Trends" in this chapter, and section on grouping adults in Chapter VII quoted from *Christian Nurture Through the Church*.)

Special Requirements

While the younger adults can readily use any part of the building, older adults should be protected against unnecessary stair climbing. Their rooms should be on the first floor, if possible. In some instances, it may be wise to install ramps, if they do not take up too much floor area or are not too difficult to install on the exterior of the building.

Special attention will need to be given to lighting for rooms used by older adults. Lighting should provide the recommended foot candle intensity at reading level, and should be free from glare, either from fixtures or from window areas.

Kitchen facilities or kitchenettes should be accessible to the rooms where adults commonly meet for their activities.

Equipment

Adult rooms should include tables for small discussion groups, serviceable, comfortable chairs (additional substantial folding chairs may well be placed in storage cabinets for use in case of special need), blackboards, lecterns, pictures, Bibles, books, a piano, cabinets and cases for supplies, adequate provision for the use of audio-visual equipment. (See Chapter XII.)

More informality in seating adults while engaged in study projects is advocated. Adherence to the activity type of floor space recommended above will permit this type of seating, and provide for a variety of undertakings which otherwise cannot be carried on in a room of lesser floor space.

A small prayer or meditation room and a good church library with a book section for adults will add greatly to the church's ministry to these elder citizens who constitute so large and so important a part of our present day population. Science has added years to their lives. The church has a solemn responsibility to help make these years meaningful and rewarding.

[1] F. Grover Fulkerson, "Older Adults in the Church," *International Journal of Religious Education* (July-August, 1954)

Summary of Space and Equipment for Adults[2]

Age Group	Maximum Persons Per Room	Floor Space Per Person	Furniture and Equipment
Young Adults Ages 24-35 Adults Ages 36-64 Older Adults 65 yrs. up	20-25 preferred 50 persons maximum	Lecture type 8-10 sq.ft. per person 10-12 sq. ft. for activity type teaching	Facilities for study groups and discussions, tables for discussion groups and study, comfortable chairs, blackboards or turn-over charts, lecterns, pictures, Bibles, books, pianos, cabinets for supplies, provision for dramatics and audio-visuals. (See Chapters 11, 12, 14.) Facilities for teas, light refreshments, suppers, hobby and recreation, and informal fellowship weekday clubs, recreation, etc. Small meditation room apart from the nave or chapel.

For Adults and Older Adults Rooms should be on first floor, if possible.

[2] Presbyterian Church in the U.S.A.

Rooms Needed in Relation to Program and to Size of Church School

Adult Division[3]

	Church School 1-99	Church School 100-299	Church School 300-499	Church School 500-899	Church School 900 and up
Young Adult	**Enrollment up to 10** Church school class may meet in sanctuary or in nearby home. Social, recreation and service activities of class, and of young adult fellowship, may use church dining room or homes of members.	**Enrollment up to 30** One classroom advisable especially for parents' class, or a mixed group. Class may use sanctuary. For other class and young adult fellowship activities in fellowship hall or other rooms, or in homes. Provision needed for dramatics, recreation, and audio-visuals.	**Enrollment up to 50** Two classrooms advisable; one for parents' group, one for a mixed group. Sanctuary pews may be used. Young adult fellowship Sunday night and week night activities in fellowship hall or other rooms, or in homes. Provision needed for dramatics, recreation, and audio-visuals.	**Enrollment up to 50** Same needs in general as medium church school, except provision for more class groupings according to interest needs. A church hobby room would enlist many young adults. Provision needed also for dramatics, recreation, and audio-visuals.	**Enrollment 100 or more** Same needs in general as large church school. More activities on Sunday night and week nights will need church space because homes cannot usually accommodate larger attendance.
Middle Adult	**Enrollment up to 10** Church school class may meet in sanctuary or nearby home. **Comments:** Middle adults will also be active in men's fellowships, women's associations, and other organized groups, and will need space and equipment for such activities. However, these meeting places will probably be used by other age groups at other times, thus making it unnecessary to build and equip these rooms for adults only. Storage space must thus be provided for equipment that will serve the different age groups.	**Enrollment up to 30** One or two class meeting places in sanctuary or available rooms in other parts of the church.	**Enrollment up to 30** Same general space and equipment needs as medium church school, with allowance for larger attendance, and provision for informal interest groups.	**Enrollment up to 50** Same general space and equipment needs as medium church school, with allowance for more classes, especially short term interest groups. (See comments on opposite page, and at bottom of this page for additional suggestions for space and equipment, and for middle adult participation in men's fellowships, women's associations, and other organized groups.)	**Enrollment 100 or more** Smaller classes of 20 to 30 preferable to one or two large classes.
Older Adult	**Enrollment up to 7** No special facilities needed. Older adults will probably participate in middle adult study and activities. (See section on "Older Adult Needs" for trends in providing special activities.)	**Enrollment up to 21** May participate with middle adults. If separate class is needed a section of the pews in the sanctuary will probably be available.	**Enrollment up to 35**	**Enrollment 65 or more**	**Enrollment up to 65** (See section on older adults in this chapter.) **Comments:** Space should also be considered for meeting of entire adult department of the church school. An office for administration of the adult department, and for records, is desirable. A fellowship hall with stage, kitchenette, provision for audio-visuals, hobbies, recreation, and service activities, will provide for a multiplicity of uses for almost every kind of adult needs.

Comments: The enrollment figures used in this chart are based on a sampling of a variety of church schools. It was found that there were approximately 27 adults to every 100 pupils enrolled in the church school. The figure 27 was broken down into 10 young adults, 10 middle adults, and 7 older adults. However, church school situations are so varied in proportionate age groupings that many exceptions must be made.

[3] Presbyterian Church in the U.S.A.

CHAPTER 12

Audio-Visual Education

The wealth of audio-visual materials now available make it possible to bring the variety and the wonder of the world into the church school classroom. Through the controlled use of these teaching tools, learning experiences can be greatly enriched. What needs to be understood is that materials and equipment must be selected and buildings planned to assure the most effective use of these powerful and promising means of education. Poor acoustics, inadequate ventilation, lack of means for light control, rooms of wrong dimension for good viewing of projected materials, improper placing of speakers, inadequate wiring, will practically nullify the educational effectiveness of audio-visual programs.

The use of audio-visuals in Christian education is just in its infancy. Increasingly, as new materials now in the making are developed and cost of production is lowered through mass production, this relatively new medium will be closely geared to the day by day teaching procedure of the church and will be used extensively. Churches planning new buildings should include the proper conduits in the construction to make effective use of audio-visual materials in every classroom. This can be done at relatively little increase in the original building cost if cared for in the planning stage.

The materials used should be definitely related to the particular curriculum of the group. They are aides, not substitutes. The materials should be used skillfully in the classroom without bungling, time-consuming improvisations, and other distractions. Audio-visuals should, as far as possible, be used within the classroom area.

The marching of children from one room to another, except in rare instances, smacks of going to the theater, disrupts the teaching continuity, and takes the pupils out of their classroom learning environment to a special projection room. Furthermore, it is more economical to make provision for darkening each classroom than to maintain and equip a special audio-visual room.

Persons charged with the responsibility of planning today's Christian educational facilities for tomorrow's needs, should be concerned to see that the best possible provision is made for the right use of audio-visuals, the promising new ally of the teacher.

Projected and Nonprojected

1. *Nonprojected materials:* These are important but often are overlooked as a part of the non-oral teaching which directly and indirectly contributes to the learning process. Nonprojected visual aids include art objects, blackboards, models, exhibits, bulletin boards, dioramas, built-up picture frames and mounts, easels for finger painting, and color pictures hung at eye level on the walls, a scene through a window, rugs, curtains, draperies, walls, floors, furniture, knickknacks. All are visible and condition the attitudes and ideas of the people who see them. Pictures and religious symbols have an uncanny way of reaching the inner lives of people and evoking gratifying religious responses. (See list of graded pictures titles in Chapter XIII.)

2. *Equipment for projected materials:* Here may be found 2″ x 2″ slide and filmstrip projectors, the 3¼″ x 4″ standard slide projectors, and the versatile opaque projectors. The latter will project drawings, pictures, and printed copy from an open book or magazine without the necessity of removing the individual pages. With those just mentioned we include 16 mm combination sound and silent motion picture projectors. Television sets are coming into use in church schools in the larger churches where funds are available for closed circuit television programs. Until such time as better programs are forthcoming from commercial stations, open circuit television programs have a limited use in churches for religious educational purposes.

Audios

Triple speed record players equipped to handle 33⅓, 45 or 78 r.p.m. recordings and a carefully selected library of records are useful in classrooms and social rooms. Many churches make excellent use of equipment designed to make recordings of music, speeches, and other programs. Magnet tape recorders are now commonly used for reproducing worship services, music, speeches, the proceedings of seminar and discussion groups and committee meetings. Shut-ins and absentees benefit particularly from the skillful use of these recordings.

Performance Standards

The very best equipment is of little value unless we can use it effectively. *How* we project materials is as important as *what* we project.

We are indebted to "Planning Schools for Use of Audio-Visual Materials," Department of Audio-Visual Instruction, National Education Association, Washington, D. C., for most of the practical suggestions which we now offer on this subject of good performance.

1. *Light Control.* No system yet devised will permit satisfactory daylight projection of pictures in the classrooms without facilities for light control. Ideally, the light reaching the screen from sources other than the projector should not exceed one-tenth foot candle intensity. This is a level of illumination which will permit reading with difficulty ordinary newspaper type. Such controlled lighting assures good picture projection and reduces eye strain from prolonged viewing of a very bright screen which contrasts too sharply with the surrounding darkness. A 25 watt lamp placed behind a screen gives a restful intermediary softness to the brightness-blackness contrast between screen and room. This will necessitate placing the screen away from the wall some eighteen inches to permit the light stand to be placed behind the screen. Even if the measurable general lighting is correct, make certain that no narrow beams of light, especially sunlight, enter the room to produce distracting bright spots.

Research reveals that where controlled lighting arrangements permit an even intensity of illumination of one foot candle throughout a small room to be directed downward from the ceiling, the intensity of the nonprojected light reaching the screen is approximately that recommended. Such a lighting arrangement affords good projection conditions and supplies sufficient illumination to permit pupils to take simple notes.

2. *Draperies, Shades, and Blinds.* The common means of light control are draperies, opaque shades (blinds), full closure Venetian blinds, and adjustable louvers.

Where draperies are used, it is recommended that they be of opaque, fire resistant plastic materials installed on tracks and equipped with a workable pull cord arrangement. Where windows are small, regular window draperies of ample fulness, if properly installed, will serve acceptably. For example, a window fifty-four inches wide requires an 81-inch width of material. Draperies can be mounted inside the casement, or on the face of the casement. Weights installed in the hems will keep the drapery steady when windows are open for ventilation. This lets in air and keeps light out. Rods and pull cords are required to assure ready, easy operation of these drapery window closures. Care should be taken to install the draperies at a sufficient distance from the window casement and the floor to permit ventilation of the room when the draperies are closed. While they cost a little more than other window coverings which we mention subsequently, draperies have acoustical and decorative values in addition to controlling outside light.

Opaque shades, if used, need special installation to insure that outdoor light does not enter the room around them. Channels of wood or metal flaps at the

sides of the windows in which the shades slide up and down, and a canopy at the top into which the shades roll when not in use, will be required for good results. Hinged wood flaps which can be turned back against the inside of the window casings are preferred to the channels as they do not fray the shades. The drawback in the use of shades is the problem of adequate window ventilation and the fact that they are not efficient for classrooms with the new type of picture windows. Ordinary house shades tend to pinhole and tear easily, and therefore the opaque material is preferred.

Venetian blinds, if they are of the full enclosure type with slats broader than the standard makes and designed to form a trap, serve to shut out light effectively, while allowing some air circulation for ventilation. Building committees, in conference with the architect, will need early in the building program to determine the type of light control system to be installed so provision can be made for its proper initial installation.

3. *Ventilation.* The importance of ventilation has been stressed repeatedly throughout this book. We shall not stress it further except to emphasize the necessity of taking precaution to insure an adequate supply of fresh air in rooms where windows are covered with opaque materials and doors are closed to control light. If attention is to be maintained at a high level, there should be a minimum replacement of room air of ten cubic feet per person per minute. Where other means are not available it may be necessary to install a reversible electric fan in a window to insure adequate ventilation. This will permit air exhaust in winter and air cooling intake in summer.

Acoustics

Satisfactory acoustic environment and good hearing should result in conditions where "the character and magnitude of all noises are compatible with the satisfactory use of the space for its intended purpose." Noise is sound which defeats this requirement. Noise intensity should not exceed thirty-five to forty decibels. This requires: (a) keeping the background noises low enough; (b) controlling the reverberation time within the room to avoid repeated overlapping of successive sounds as they bound from one room surface to another and yet at the same time assuring some blending; (c) controlling the noise from adjoining spaces. The desired effect can be reached inexpensively by applying sound-absorbing materials on the interior of the room, by locating the classroom away from noisy areas of the building, by acoustically treating corridors and mechanical installations within the building, and by the use of good wall and door materials. Acoustical treatment of the ceiling is usually adequate for rooms of 1,000 to 1,200 square feet. Larger rooms may need additional treatment.

It should be noted that a room, while satisfactory for some purposes, may yet so deaden sound as to make music distracting and lacking in resonance. The best procedure is to plan properly when the building is being erected, and to use a competent architect and/or an acoustical engineer both for new buildings and the correction of unsatisfactory existing conditions.

Speakers

As a general rule, speakers should not be permanently installed in the walls of classrooms for the reasons that: (1) they tend to decrease in efficiency with use; (2) not every speaker will match the output of all types of equipment. It is better to install a bracket or drop shelf which will fold against the wall when not in use, and which is of sufficient size to hold any normal speaker. In small rooms the speaker can be set on the back of the room near the projector. This will eliminate stringing long cables about the room, if proper conduits have not been installed.

Electrical Installations

These consist of: (1) the wiring, switches, and outlets for the projection of silent and sound materials and the proper lighting and light control within the room; (2) the installations required for radio and television, especially closed television circuits.

1. *Switches:* In addition to silent switches accessibly placed near doorways for control of overhead lighting, an additional switch should be installed on the wall opposite the side of the room on which the projection screen is mounted. This makes possible easy and immediate control of room lights by the person operating the projector.

2. *Outlets:* Three double outlets should be installed in each room; one each at the back, front, and side of the room. One outlet should be near the usual location of the projection stand. Outlets at the front will care for overhead projectors, record players, and tape recorders. Outlets at the side of the room will be used for small group work.

3. *Wiring:* Lines serving these outlets should be on separate circuits from those serving the regular overhead lighting system. Wiring and outlets should conform to safety code requirements, deliver 110 volt alternating current, be fused for not less than 20 amperes, and circuits installed to permit simultaneous use of equipment in any number of rooms without overloading the electric lines within the building.

4. *Speaker Conduit:* A ¾-inch conduit should be permanently installed to feed the sound energy from the projector to the speaker. One outlet for the speaker line should be placed near the projector and a companion outlet near the speaker's stand. This eliminates hazards to pupils and equipment caused by the pupils tripping over cables running across floor areas.

Radio and Television

The rapid development and the educational possibilities of these media make it imperative that our larger churches erecting new buildings should make provision for their use. This entails the counsel of an expert in this field. Briefly, we indicate some basic items which can be installed readily and at comparatively low cost while the church edifice is under construction.

Central Sound Conduit: The installation of 1¼-inch inside diameter conduit will permit later insertion of a coaxial cable for television use. The outlet from this conduit should be installed in the front of the room near the place where equipment will be located and wiring installations completed for the use of television.

Radio and Television Antennae: A ¾-inch conduit should be installed leading from the master antennae for radio and television to the room or rooms where these programs are to be presented. This conduit should carry the antennae, ground wire and booster circuit, and be installed so that a standard receptacle can be plugged into the rooms involved. Where neither commercial nor outside programs are to be used at present, television antennae may be omitted temporarily. We again indicate the wisdom of planning well in advance with the help of an expert. Putting in electric conduits after the bulding is completed is a costly business, and usually results in inferior installation.

Projection Screens: The screen selected for classroom projection should be easily set up and readily stored to protect it from dirt and damage. Some persons prefer a pull-down screen in an inconspicuous roller case mounted on the wall. Others will favor a flat mounted screen behind a movable chalkboard or bulletin board. Tripod mounted screens have many advantages but are space consuming and accident hazardous. A special paint for a classroom wall surface provides a reasonably satisfactory projection surface.

Size: For all types of projection in the larger sized classrooms now recommended, a 70-inch by 70-inch screen is preferable. At a distance of 30 feet a 16 mm. projector using a two-inch lens, or a 35 mm. filmstrip projector using a five-inch lens, will practically fill this screen. Square screens will take a variety of picture shapes including opaque projected materials, and are therefore recommended. A smaller screen of not less than fifty inches in width can be used, provided it is not farther away from the viewers than five times the width of the screen image.

Projection screens for small groups of six to twelve pupils may be much smaller. Screens thirty-six inches square and mounted in a spring roller case are satisfactory for such groups.

Realizing that rooms vary in size from a small classroom i.e., twelve by fifteen feet, to large parish halls, i.e., forty-five by seventy-five feet and more, we offer the following tables indicating the combination of lenses and screens to be used under varying conditions:

For 16 mm. projection:

If the distance from the screen to the projector equals the distance set forth in the first horizontal

Focal Length of lens	1'	2'	3'	4'	5'	6'	8'	10'	15'	20'	30'	40'	50'	75'	100'	150'
						Width of Picture										
1"	4"	9"	13"	18"	22"	27"	36"	45"	5'8"	7'7"	11'4"	15'2"	19'0"			
2"	2"	4"	6"	9"	11"	13"	18"	22"	34"	45"	5'8"	7'7"	9'6"	14'3"	19'0"	28'5"
3"		3"	4"	6"	7"	9"	12"	15"	22"	30"	45"	5'0"	6'4"	9'6"	12'8"	19'0"

35 MM PROJECTION (Slide)   Distance from screen in feet

Focal Length of lens	Type of Slide	1'	2'	3'	4'	5'	6'	8'	10'	15'	20'	30'	40'	50'	75'	100'	150'
								Width of Picture									
2"	S-35*	5"	10"	15"	21"	26"	32"	43"	53"	6'9"	9'0"	13'6"	18'1"	22'7"	34'0"		
5"	S-35*		3"	6"	8"	10"	12"	16"	21"	32"	43"	5'4"	7'2"	9'0"	13'6"	18'1"	27'1"
7"	S-35*			4"	5"	7"	8"	12"	15"	22"	30"	46"	5'1"	6'5"	9'8"	12'10"	19'4"
2"	D-35†	7"	15"	23"	31"	39"	49"	5'3"	6'7"	9'11"	13'3"	20'0"	26'8"	33'4"			
5"	D-35†		5"	8"	12"	15"	17"	24"	31"	49"	5'3"	7'11"	10'7"	13'3"	20'0"	26'8"	
7"	D-35†		3"	5"	8"	10"	12"	17"	22"	33"	45"	5'7"	7'7"	9'5"	14'3"	19'0"	28'7"

*S-35 — Single frame filmstrips   †D-35 — 2 x 2 slides and double frame filmstrips

(Chart is from "Using Audio-Visuals in the Church," Division of Christian Education, National Council of Churches, and is used by permission.)[1] The most pleasing results are obtained by filling the screen with the projected image.

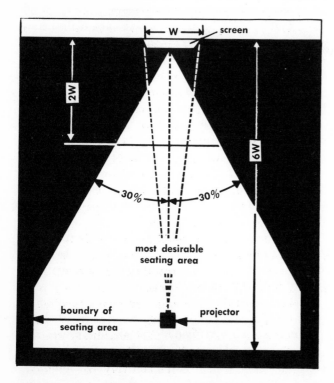

The viewing angle, or boundary of satisfactory seating area, in relation to the screen must be limited to 30 degrees. Picture width should be 1/6 distance from last row of seats. First row should not be closer to screen than twice its width.

line of feet figures in the charts above, and the focal length of the lens used is that in the first lefthand vertical column, the results in terms of picture width will be found in the horizontal lines opposite the lens-length figures.

Location: The screen should be placed so that the lower edge is at eye level of the seated pupils. No installation such as ceiling lights should interfere with the viewing. (See paragraph on Performance Standards—Light Control). The screen should be placed so as to be readily seen from all parts of the pupil seating area, and at no greater angle than 30 degrees from a line perpendicular to the center of the screen. No viewer should sit farther from the screen than six times the image width nor closer than two times the image width. For these reasons a reasonably narrow room is better for projection audio-visuals than an extremely wide room.

Screen Types

There are three types of screens: (1) the white matte screen; (2) the beaded screen, and (3) the daylight type screen.

1. *The Matte Screens* have smooth surfaces and are preferred for use in square classrooms for the

reason that there is less distortion from all parts of the room than with the beaded screen.

2. *Beaded Screens:* These are surfaced with small glass beads and consequently reflect a higher proportion of the projected light to the viewer near the center of the room.

3. *Daylight Screens:* Several of these screens permit fairly satisfactory projection of pictures in small classrooms where light control is lacking. In this group are found (a) the hooded or box-type screen (b) the

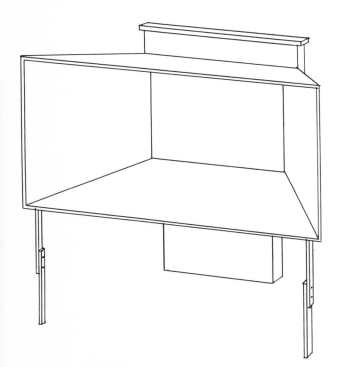

Hooded Screen for Daylight Projection

This screen can be placed upon a table. The screen is at the back of the enclosure. The panels top, bottom, and sides partially reduce the daylight and permit a brighter image on the screen.

rear projection screen. By means of this the picture is projected from behind and through a translucent screen. In small groups, this is quite effective and permits the person operating the projector to face the class directly and to view the pictures he is showing.

Projection Stands

A good projection stand is useful, adaptable, and a much needed piece of equipment for good operation of projectors, tape recorders, record players, radios, and other objects for use in the classroom. A good stand needs to be sturdy enough to carry eighty-five to one hundred pounds, steady enough to withstand the vibration of a 16 mm. sound projector, and some four and a half feet above the floor. The top should measure not less than twelve by twenty-four inches. Shelves and hooks for cables and film can pockets will add to its usefulness. The stand should be mounted on three-fourths-inch-rubber-tired wheels and equipped with a brake so it will stay in position.

The "make-it-yourself" stands illustrated below are not up to the standards just recommended, but will serve acceptably for light weight projection equipment.

Storage Facilities

To preserve materials from dirt and damage and to make possible their classification for ready use, each church should provide a central storage space equipped with storage cabinets for objects varying in size and shape. In the average church there will be flat pictures, charts, posters, filmstrips and slides, and projection equipment. Larger churches will need to plan for film library space, previewing, auditioning, and repairing films, and the storage of a variety of valuable equipment. Currently used nonprojected materials will be kept in the classroom; projection equipment should be stored in an audio-visual center or headquarters for the whole church. Detailed information and illustrations on audio-visual equipment

Projection Stands

Left: Filmstrip projection; right: motion-pictures. These stands have three special features: height; three legs, to stand solid; work-shelf for reel cans, etc.

The smaller is for a filmstrip projector. It is 47½ inches high, weighs 8½ pounds and is made of oak, except for the work shelf, which is of plywood. The top shelf is 7¾ by 15¾ inches; the work shelf, 9¾ by 18 inches. The larger stand is for a heavy-duty motion picture projector. It is 50 inches high, and weighs 16 pounds. The legs are oak, and the shelves ¾ inch plywood. The top shelf is 13 by 18 inches; the work shelf, 16 x 20 inches.

(Courtesy of International Journal of Religious Education)

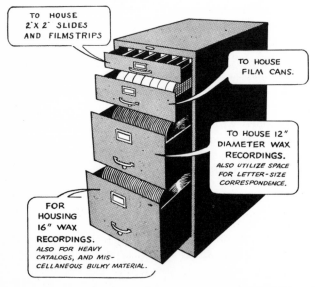

All-Purpose Filing Cabinets for Audio-Visual Material

storage may be found in Booklet No. 3, Audio-Visual Instructional Materials Center, Department of Audio-Visual Instruction, National Education Association, Washington, D. C.

A Beginning

The Green Lake Workshop on Audio-Visual and Church Building (1955) suggested the purchase of basic equipment by churches in the following order:

1. a screen
2. a slide-film projector
   (a high wattage projector will give better results in daylight conditions)
3. a three speed record player
4. magnetic tape recorder
5. 16 mm. sound projector
6. movable equipment—stands, etc.
7. opaque projector
8. lenses of various lengths
9. overhead projector

Larger churches will undoubtedly need to provide a number of pieces of equipment and to develop an extensive library of slides, filmstrips, and films as budgets permit and satisfactory new materials become available.

Audio-Visuals in the Small Church

Attention is directed to the section on Audio-Visuals in Chapter XVII.

In addition to seeking the advice of experts in this comparatively new and rapidly developing field, church committees will be rewarded by reading the publications listed in the appended bibliography:

Using Audio-Visuals in the Church, Division of Christian Education, National Council of Churches. Available from the Office of Publication and Distribution, 120 E. 23rd Street, New York 10, New York. Price 75¢.

Planning Schools for Use of Audio-Visual Materials, Book No. 1, *Classrooms;* No. 2, *Auditoriums,* No. 3, *Audio-Visual Instructional Materials Center* Department of Audio-Visual Instruction, National Educational Association, 1201 Sixteenth Street, N. W., Washington, D. C., price $1.00 for each booklet.

Many articles in issues of *International Journal of Religious Education,* 257 Fourth Ave., New York 10, N. Y. See special issue November, 1957, "Built-in Audio-Visuals," and "Audio-Visual Specifications in Church Architecture."

CHAPTER 13

Art in the Service of Christian Education

Art is language. Tolstoi called it the language of emotion. Great art speaks a language of its own and conveys from the soul of the artist to those who view his work those profound emotions which "break through language and escape."

As Albert Edward Bailey reminds us in "The Gospel in Art," that "though the human voice is soon silent and the human heart will one day grow cold, yet because the artist's kind of speech is permanent he can transmit his passions endlessly as long as there are spectators to pass before his canvas."[1] The insights, the imagery and the idealism of the vast heritage of Christian art rightly used have much to offer in the furtherance of Christian education. Youth, if schooled in this heritage, can acquire a growing appreciation of this treasury of religious inspiration.

Symbols

While the study of this vast field is richly rewarding to adults, symbolism has little value for children. For this reason, symbols are being omitted from children's classrooms. Beauty in the decor of their rooms, in the simple objects which belong to their experience, in pictures graded to their understanding is much more meaningful than the traditional symbols of the Christian Church. A clear glass window which lets in the sunlight and permits a view of the world of growing things is far better for them than the heavy colored pictured or figured opaque glass which has characterized so many windows of church buildings of the past. The dim religious light may have its place and the medieval symbols their value, but they are not for children.

Music

Music is a very important part of the curriculum of Christian education. Religion and music go hand in hand and appeal to all ages. Music provides a social as well as a religious experience and brings people together, feeds their minds, stirs their emotions, brings them together in offering their praise and thanksgiving to God. Carefully chosen music can induce almost any desired mood, particularly that of reverence. Music should be chosen with great care as to its quality, the content of the hymns and songs, the range of the voices

in each age group, and with consideration for the needs of each age level. The words should give accurate ideas that a young child can understand and there should be no symbolism.

In her book, *Guiding Children in Christian Growth*, Mary Alice Jones reminds us: "There are now available excellent collections of children's songs for the various age groups. The symbolic hymns of the past generation, such as 'Rock of Ages,' 'Lead Kindly Light,' 'There Is a Fountain Filled with Blood,' have no place in the children's departments. And the so-called 'Gospel hymns' of more recent days sometimes express strange theology and often phrase expressions in verse which lack the inspiring quality of great poetry. It is wiser for the sake of the child's Christian growth to use songs and hymns which express in simple, well chosen words the joys of living in God's world, the happiness of human fellowship, the response to the great affirmations of the Christian faith in terms of friendly, brotherly conduct, and the aspiration of man to be a worthy child of God and a true disciple of Jesus Christ."[2]

Needless to say the musical instruments in the church school should be in tune and in good repair, and we hope kept free from the weird paint which is frequently applied to what would otherwise be an attractive feature of the particular room. Piano keys should be clean and the instrument uncluttered with tattered music or other encumbrances. Song and hymnbooks should be chosen with far greater care than obtains in many schools. By the time a child has reached the junior age he can, if properly trained, have a real appreciation of good music and a knowledge of the meaning and beauty of many of the best hymns of the church.

Record players and records which are now being used increasingly should also receive the most careful consideration as to their quality and mechanical effectiveness.

A large easel with large sheets of sturdy paper or cardboard can be used to display large script letters of the words to be sung. This will serve to focus attention especially in children's groups and, where funds are limited, will permit the purchase of at least one good book of songs for each age group.

Pictures

The right use of good religious pictures can make an invaluable contribution to the religious life of the church school. "They present to the eye," says Cynthia Pearl Maus in *Christ and the Fine Arts*, "what would take much longer to tell to the ear . . . a truth which reaches the mind through the eye-gate and the ear-gate doubles the impression."[3] They should be carefully selected and graded to the ages of the pupils for which they are suited. A few really beautiful pictures are to be preferred to a large collection of inferior, crudely colored, garish creations.

Each room should have one picture of real quality hung at eye level on the clear expanse of an unbroken wall. It will give a spiritual character to the whole room and often reach into the depths of many a human spirit. A frame which can be opened from the back will permit changing of pictures from time to time as required. The skillful teacher will gather pictures from all available sources and by mounting them on cardboard can preserve them for use as needed. A cabinet space should be designed and provided to store these pictures.

A beautiful picture placed above a low table can be used as a religious interest center in the children's rooms. Art galleries in some communities will lend religious pictures to churches for adult use.

The following is a partial list of pictures classified for the several age groups of the church school:

For the Nursery Department

Spring of the Year—Muriel Dawson
Floral Procession—French Poster
Spring Song—Glucklich
Song of the Bluebird—Kenyon
Suffer Little Children—Tarrant
Madonna and Child—Raphael
Jessie Wilcox Smith pictures—Simple pictures illustrating child life, animals and flowers.
Mother and Child—Kollwitz
Child with Dove—Picasso
Christ Blessing Children—Remmey

For the Kindergarten Department

(Any of the above—if not already purchased)

Morning Carol—Tarrant
Youthful Gardeners—Middorigh-Bokhorst
Rabbits—Muriel Dawson
Spring—Cizek
Arrival of the Shepherds—Lerolle
Sistine Madonna (Detail only)—Raphael
The Holy Family—Elsie Anna Wood
Suffer Little Children—Tarrant
Good Friends—Muriel Dawson

For the Primary Department

When All the World Was Young—Tarrant
He Prayeth Best—Tarrant
Spring—Cizek
The Arrival of the Shepherds—Lerolle
Of Such Is the Kingdom—Elsie Anna Wood
The Hilltop at Nazareth—Elsie Anna Wood
The Sermon on the Mount—Elsie Anna Wood

Workshop at Nazareth—Briggs
Mary and the Shepherd Boy—Scheurenberg
Jesus and the Children—Katz
Madonna—Ferruzzi
The Angelus—Millet
Madonna of the Chair—Raphael
The Sisters—Taylor
Madonna and Child—Murillo
Christ Blessing Little Children—Plockhorst
Nativity—Baroccio
Madonna Granduca—Raphael
The Friend—Elsie Anna Wood
The Holy Family—Elsie Anna Wood
The Carpenter Shop in Nazareth—Tarrant

For the Junior Department

St. Francis Preaching to the Birds—Giotto
The Angelus—Millet
The Children's Hour—Taylor
Christ and the Doctors—Hofmann
Jesus in the Midst of the Doctors—Seignac
The Harvest Moon—Tarrant
Reading Wycliffe's Bible—Clausen
Pilgrims Going to Church—Boughton
Christ and the Fisherman—Zimmerman
Jesus and the Children—Copping
Christ and the Rich Young Ruler—Hofmann
The Boy Jesus—Murillo
Arrival of the Shepherds—Lerolle
O Little Town of Bethlehem—Taylor
When I Consider Thy Heavens—Taylor
Peter and John—Burnand
The Last Supper—DaVinci
The Hilltop at Nazareth—Elsie Anna Wood
Moses—Michelangelo
The Head of Christ—Barosin
The Teacher—Elsie Anna Wood
The Last Supper—Derain
Jesus Going Into Wilderness to Pray—Hole
The Carpenter Shop—Barosin

For Youth or Adults

The Remorse of Judas—Armitage
The Builder—Beneker
Calling of Matthew—Bidd
The Presence—Borthwick
Jesus Washes the Disciples' Feet—Brown
Peter and John—Burnand
The Builder—Burnand
Christ of the Andes—Cimabui
Madonna—Cimabui
Christ Appearing to Mary Magdalene—DaVinci
The Last Supper—DaVinci
Christ Weeping over the City—Flandrin
The Walk to Emmaus—Gerardet
St. Francis Feeding the Birds—Giotto
Jesus and Zacchaeus—Hardy
Christ and the Rich Young Ruler—Hofmann
Christ and the Young People—Hofmann
Christ in Gethsemane—Hofmann
Christ Among the Lowly—Lhermite
The Angelus—Millet
Prodigal Song—Molitor
Trial Before Pilate—Munkacsy
Christ's Complaint to the Nations—Raemaeker
Omnipresence—Rosencraz
Christ Blessing the Meal—Von Uhde
Prodigal's Return—Schafer
Holy Family—Seligmann
When I Consider Thy Heavens—Taylor

The Prodigal's Return—Tissot
Tribute Money—Titian
Sermon on the Mount—Wood
Christ and the Fisherman—Zimmerman
The Great Commission—Barosin
Head of Christ—Barosin
Christ Washing Peter's Feet—Brown
Peter and John Running to the Tomb—Burnand
Ecce Homo—Ciseri
The Saviour—Coleman
Jesus and the Children—Copping
Crucifix—Dali
The Christ of St. John—Dali
Praying Hands—Durer
The Hands—Durer
A Modern Madonna—Feruzzi
Jesus and the Children—Flandrin
Peter's Denial—Harrick
Thy Kingdom Come—Larson
Repose in Egypt—Merson
Last Supper—Rembrandt
Man's Controlling Nature—Rivira
Benediction—Roualt
Descent From the Cross—Rubens
The Lost Sheep—Soord
Sermon on the Mount—Uhde
For He Had Great Possessions—Watts
Prodigal's Return—Wood

Dramatics

Currently there are intimations of a renewed interest in dramatics in the educational programs of our churches. In an article, "Using Role Playing in Christian Education," by Charles L. Burns, Jr., in the *International Journal of Religious Education*,[5] the author introduces us to the value and techniques of role-playing as a useful educational instrument. While little equipment is needed for its furtherance, adequate floor space in classrooms is necessary to permit this method of learning. Chapter XV deals in detail with the more formal approaches to dramatic presentations. Caution: In many instances staging can be informal, portable and relatively inexpensive, which at the same time allows for the use of dramatics in Christian education.

Painting and the Plastic Arts

Finger painting, the use of water colors and crayons have an important place when properly used in the educational procedures of the understanding teacher. The same can be said of the use of the plastic materials now available for classroom use. The wise and sympathetic educator will include these therapeutic and creative means with others for the furtherance of the teaching ministry of the church.

[1] Albert Edward Bailey, *The Gospel in Art* (Pilgrim Press, 1931)
[2] Mary Alice Jones, *Guiding Children in Christian Growth* (Abingdon-Cokesbury, 1949)
[3] Cynthia Pearl Maus, *Christ in the Fine Arts* (Harper and Brothers, 1938)
[4] List of pictures revised May, 1958, after consultation with official representatives of the following committees of the N.C.C.C.U.S.A.: Children's Work, Youth Work, Adult Work. This list is a guide for selection of pictures. There is no single source for their purchase. Consult public libraries or art museums, denominational publishing houses, or commercial distributors. The National Council of Churches *does not sell* the above pictures.
[5] Charles L. Burns, "Using Role Playing in Christian Education," *International Journal of Religious Education* (reprint available)

NOTE: Special issue "*Art in Christian Education*," published by the *International Journal of Religious Education*, February 1959 is an excellent resource and contains many full color reproductions as well as black and white photographs of great ancient and modern art. Available from the International Journal as follows: 1-9 copies—.75¢; 10-49 copies—.50¢; 50 or more copies—.40¢.

CHAPTER 14

Providing for Administrative and Building Maintenance Requirements................

Efficiently planned, accessibly located, and well equipped administration space is a necessary adjunct to the program of Christian education. Adequately planned and equipped office space will increase the efficiency and effect economies in the work of the trained staff and volunteer leadership.

Rooms

1. The general office or offices should be near the principal weekday entrance for accessibility and control of traffic in and out of the building. The general office staff should be protected from the public, either by a counter placed between the working area and the public, or a door, the upper half of which is glazed with clear glass and can be readily opened, while the bottom half, topped with a narrow shelf, provides a low barrier.

2. A work room adjacent to the church office will be required for supplies, operating duplication and addressing machines, and extra filing cabinets.

3. The pastor's study should be accessible, preferably by way of the church office, but secluded from unnecessary calls. The pastor's room should be attractively furnished, and ample provision should be made for bookshelves, storage of gowns and other appurtenances used by clergymen, and with a desk, a comfortable chair, a dictating machine, filing cabinets, a few well chosen religious pictures, and other informal chairs and furnishings. If this room is to be used for personal counseling, it should be ample in area, and so appointed as to put persons conferring with the pastor at ease. Churches with a large membership will need to provide a reception area where callers can be cared for while awaiting their appointments with members of the church staff.

4. Offices for other members of the staff—the director of Christian education, ministerial assistants, etc.—should be accessible and adjacent to the church offices to assure efficient teamwork.

5. The church library should be in a quiet, easily reached part of the building. Provision should be made for reference books, records, pictures, maps, filing cabinets, and display of current periodicals. There will need to be space for reading tables and informal chairs, shelves for workers' library and for religious books for general distribution, and exhibit cabinets for special displays. Other displays can be exhibited in glazed, well lighted, built-in wall cabinets placed in the corridors of the church school building.

6. The custodian, the hard working individual with a multitude of demands upon him, should have a room to serve as an office, and he should also be provided with space for a work bench, tools, a comfortable chair, a reading lamp and, if possible, television or radio by means of which he can entertain himself while awaiting the conclusion of prolonged evening meetings at the church.

7. A board or conference room accessible, and equipped with a large table and suitable chairs, will be found most useful. If placed next to the church office, it can be used to supplement that space when extra room is needed for collating literature or implementing special campaigns being promoted by the church. Provision should be made for the storage and possibly the use of audio-visual education equipment in this room. However, there is need for a separate

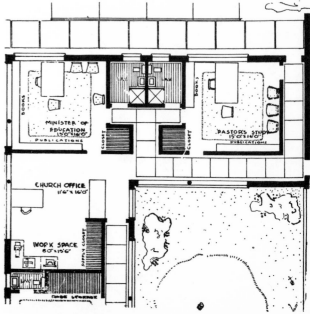

PLAN FOR GROUP OF ADMINISTRATIVE ROOMS

room where films, filmstrips, slides, etc. can be recorded and filed and equipment maintained.

General Equipment

1. *Toilets:* While previous reference has been made to these installations, emphasis again is placed upon the necessity for careful study as to location, adequacy, and sanitary conditions for these facilities. For the most part, church toilet facilities are far from satisfactory, and should be given proper attention.

A powder room for women and a small lounge for the men adjacent to at least one of each of their toilet rooms will serve to care for emergency illness. First aid cabinets whose contents have been selected by a competent medical authority should be placed in an accessible place in each of these rooms. Make certain that entrances to men's and women's facilities are not immediately adjacent to each other. Where possible, private toilet installations should be made available for the pastor and for the church staff.

2. *Heating, Ventilation, Airconditioning:* These installations should be zone-controlled to permit the office areas, in more constant use than the building as a whole, to be serviced without involving the whole building. These mechanical installations, together with the electrical equipment, should be so placed and acoustically treated as to eliminate any possible sound nuisance emanating from them.

3. *Storage Space:* Storage space and yet more such space is essential for efficiency in the operation of a church building, and particularly in furthering the Christian educational program of the church. Adequate provision needs to be made for hats and coats in convenient locations, for the storage of extra chairs and tables, and for the convenient location of the janitor's equipment such as slop bowls, floor cleaning materials, extension cords, and other equipment which may be needed on special occasions in specified areas.

4. *Adequate telephone service* with connections from the central office to the staff areas, and a public telephone accessible to the church members should also be incorporated in the general equipment of the church.

A general intercommunication system for all of the rooms in the building is not recommended. Consideration may well be given to installing an electronic communication system between the nave of the church and the fellowship hall to take care of the few special occasions when large overflow crowds need to be served. Conduits or chancel space for audio and spoken outlets can be provided in each room at a minimal cost when new building or complete remodeling is done.

Typewriters, addressing machines, duplicating equipment, card indexes, directories, ample storage cabinets, files, shelving, tables, desks, and chairs, should be provided for the efficient working of the church staff, especially in churches with a large constituency.

Cheerful, pleasing decor and good lighting, with an outside exposure, should be afforded those who spend many long working hours in the church building.

Direction signs both outside and inside the building should clearly indicate the location of the church offices. Any person who has tried to find the church office in many of our church buildings will readily concur in this important admonition.

The following chart covering the administrative functions of the church, prepared by the Presybyterian Church, U.S.A., sets forth in readily understood detail, suggested standards of equipment for churches of various sizes:

Rooms Needed in Relation to Program and to Size of Church School

Administrative Functions [1]

Persons and Functions	Church School 1–99	Church School 100–299	Church School 300–499	Church School 500–899	Church School 900 and up
Pastor	Study and work room. Built-in table and shelves with curtain or doors to conceal mimeograph equipment when not in use.	Study and separate work room. Closet for supplies.	Study and office for secretary with equipment for records. Work room with cabinets for supplies.	Study with office for secretary. Office for church secretary. Offices for other staff members and their secretaries. Work room and supply closets.	Same as for 500-899 church school with addition of Conference or Board room adequate for largest group, should have table, exhibit space, blackboard, A-V equipment.
Director of Christian Education	None.	None.	Office large enough for desk, table, bookcases, and chairs. Space for counseling and small committee work.	Office large enough for desk, table, bookcases, chairs, with space for counseling and committee work. A separate office for secretary.	Same as for 500-899 church school plus offices for age-group assistants and their secretaries.
Church School Supt., Secretary & Treasurer	Desk space with shelves or chest of drawers for literature, supplies, and records.	Room with desks and cabinets for records, literature and supplies.	Room with desks, cabinets for records, literature and supplies.	Room with desks, work table, filing cabinet for records. Storeroom for literature and supplies.	Same as for 500-899 church school but with increased space.
Choir Director	Desk or table space. Cabinet for filing church music. Closet or cabinet for choir robes.	Room with desk or table. Cabinets for music and choir robes. Shelves for hymnals used by choir.	Office with desk, cabinet and piano. Room with table, and cabinets for music, choir robes, hymnals.	Office and studio with piano. Room for robing of choir with cabinets for music, robes, and hymns.	Same as for 500-899 church school but with more ample robe closets and robing space.
Library	Built-in bookcases with locks, or space for movable units. Filing cabinet for records.	Room with bookcases (built-in or movable), table, chairs, filing cabinet for records. Cabinet for picture files.	Room with bookcases, table, chairs, cabinets for records, filing pictures and maps. Exhibit cabinets.	Large room with tables, chairs, with space for reading and study. Picture and map files. Cabinet for records. World friendship museum.	Same as for 500-899 church school but with increased space and equipment.

1 Presbyterian Church in the U.S.A.

CHAPTER 15

Providing for Recreation, Dramatics, and Fellowship

A well rounded church program will include provision for guided wholesome recreation, dramatics, and opportunities for fellowship at every age level of its constituency. The sudden uprooting of our people and the mobility of our population bring many new people into most of our church communities. These folks confront the church with a real human need, and a great opportunity. Informal occasions for recreation and fellowship are recognized as being increasingly important in weaving these new people into patterns of friendship and co-operation, and useful activity. Thereby they are ultimately brought into the working fellowship of the Christian Church. The variety of purposeful activities, and the possibilities in grouping these people in meaningful, creative, informal fellowship is practically unlimited.

The parish hall need no longer be the traditional dingy, dark brown gloom factory with its musty odor, flaking paint, and forbidding, battered interior and bad acoustics. Modern means of artificial ventilation and air conditioning make it possible to reduce considerably the cubage which was otherwise necessary to assure sufficient air for human consumption in large gatherings of people. Modern lighting installed in horizontal panels flush with the ceiling give the appearance of added height, and assure an even distribution of adequate light without glare, and without obstructing fixtures. Modern floor tile in a variety of patterns and colors and a great variety of color tones in paints and wall fabrics, make it possible to convert even the dingiest basement area into a room with cheerful decor. The tough textured vinyl plastic fabrics now available can be readily cemented to walls, to make attractive and durable surfaces adequate to withstand hard usage, yet pleasing and cheerful in appearance. Modern decorative acoustical materials for ceilings and wall panels, where such are required, make it possible to overcome the deficiencies which have so frequently handicapped the parish halls of the past.

To assure the utmost in efficiency, the stage, the kitchen, and the storage facilities, and the fellowship hall should be carefully planned as an integrated unit.

Size and Proportions

The size of the fellowship room will necessarily depend upon the program pattern adopted by the church, the size of the church membership, and, to some extent, upon the resources available. As a minimum, the size of this room should be based upon providing for one person out of every five people of the maximum designed capacity of the particular building. There should be an unobstructed floor area of from ten to twelve square feet per person, when seated at tables, or eight to ten square feet per person when seated in formal rows of chairs facing the stage or platform. Thus, a room measuring thirty feet by fifty feet will seat approximately 150 persons at tables, or approximately 185 persons in formal rows of seats.

In furtherance of good acoustics, good vision of the stage, and the most effective projection of audio-visual materials, the parish hall should be rectangular in shape, with the stage or platform across one of the narrower sides of the room. Proportions of two feet in length to one foot in width, or five feet in length to three feet in width, provide satisfactory proportions.

Now that the trend is away from the use of church facilities for basketball and heavy athletic events, ceiling heights in the fellowship hall can be kept much lower than heretofore. The ceiling height of nine feet six inches to ten feet in the clear under ceiling beams, is sufficient height for a room approximately thirty feet by fifty feet. In larger rooms, ceiling heights may need to be ten feet or twelve feet, or even more. It is advisable to keep ceiling heights as low as possible, especially where the fellowship hall is below ground, or where it is necessary to climb stairways to reach such a room on an upper floor. Every foot of ceiling height which, all things considered, can be eliminated, reduces by two the number of stair steps which have to be climbed. This is a matter of real importance where older adults are concerned. Where land use and budget permit, the fellowship hall should be erected on grade. This eliminates climbing steps, and permits daylight illumination through adequate window areas.

In many instances, it is found advisable to install a movable partition such as the Modernfold or its equivalent by means of which the hall can be divided into two rooms. Thus divided, a more intimate fellowship can be provided for smaller groups.

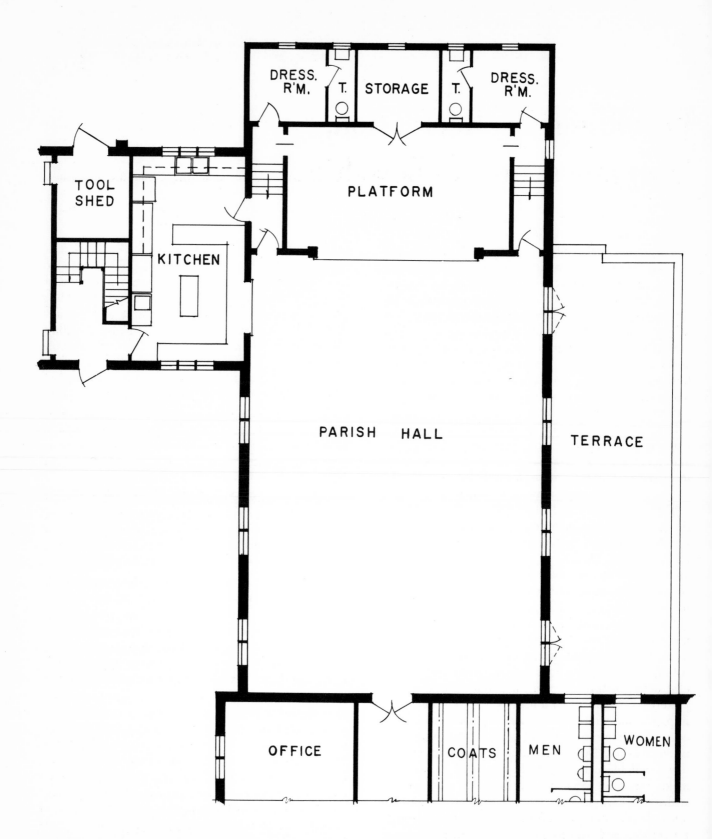

Lighting, Decoration, and Acoustics

These important subjects definitely related to the fellowship hall, are dealt with in detail in Chapters III, V, VI, and XII. To the general principles set forth in those chapters, we add the fact that the parish hall needs to have adequate visibility, both from the point of view of seeing the stage properly, and of being able to read printed programs or to participate in group activities with sufficient light to make good reading possible. The lighting should also provide a fitting atmosphere and enhance the decoration of the room so as to make it as attractive and useful as possible. The light intensity should be equal to at least ten foot candles for general assembly purposes, and should provide not less than twenty foot candles at table height, when adults are called upon to read printed materials. The general lighting for the parish hall should be controlled by dimmers so dramatic events, recitals or audio-visual programs can be cared for adequately. The stage lighting control system, when properly planned, can be tied into the dimming equipment of the fellowship hall, and thereby make it possible through that installation to control the stage lights during the performance of a play.

The Stage

To assure efficient dramatic procedures, and to sustain the interest of those involved, it is essential to plan the stage and its equipment very carefully. Otherwise, interest in dramatics will lag, and the original investment become a liability instead of an asset.

Inasmuch as the proscenium opening centers the attention of the audience upon the stage, it should not be ornately decorated, but left plain and unobtrusive. The size of the opening must necessarily be determined by a study of the sight lines run from the areas in which the audience is seated to the stage. The size of the fellowship hall and the ceiling height will also be governing factors. Ideally, the width of the proscenium opening should not be less than twenty-four feet, and with a height of twelve feet. The minimum distance from the proscenium opening (curtain line) to the rear wall of the stage, should be twenty feet. The distance between the sides of the proscenium opening and the side walls of the stage should be a minimum of twelve feet. This means then, that with the proscenium opening of twenty-four feet, the total width of the stage area would be forty-eight feet. These are ideal dimensions, and will serve as a guide to rooms of lesser width and of lower ceiling heights.

In any case, sufficient space should be provided on either side of the stage for wings to permit easy exits and entrances from the sides. There should also be depth enough to allow room for stage action and for passage back of the rear screen so the participants can make their entrances and exits from the rear.

The height of the ceiling above the stage is as important as the floor area itself. Unless a church has an exceedingly active drama group, the planning of a stage loft with gridiron and counterweight flying system would be unwise. However, even with a small stage, space must be provided for hanging curtains, scenery, and lighting instruments. To put a finished ceiling above the stage is a needless expense, and complicates the installation of equipment for hanging curtains and scenery. Likewise, a floor that is too highly finished handicaps the nailing of flats or scenery to the floor of the stage. The floor should be finished in a soft wood which will readily take nails or screws by means of which the scenery is sometimes fastened to the floor. The ceiling of the stage should be unfinished, and should have attached to and suspended from it, furring strips or slats to which scenery can be attached.

The following is a list of essentials required for the flexible use of a stage. Additional equipment will be required when the stage is used extensively:

1. A fire curtain is an asbestos cloth curtain that hangs between the proscenium opening and the stage curtain itself. This is required in most communities by the building code.

2. The act, or front curtain, is the predominant feature of the fellowship hall, and should be hung from traverse tracks in such a way as to permit opening from the center towards either side. It should be satisfying in appearance, reliable, quiet, and smooth in operation. Nothing so defeats the effectiveness of dramatic presentations as faulty lighting controls or a curtain which balks at critical points in the program.

3. The proscenium framing equipment consists of cloth elements that can be used to vary the height and the width of the opening. The height can be varied by what is called "a teaser," hanging immediately behind the act or front curtain of the stage. This item should be lined with asbestos cloth as a safety measure. The width of the opening is easily varied by pulling the stage or front curtain to a pre-determined distance from either side of the proscenium opening. Otherwise two long narrow cloth units known as "tormentors," one on each side of the stage, are hung from short traverse tracks located between the front curtain and the so-called "teasers."

Stage Lighting

Unless the audience is able to see clearly the actors on the stage, the whole purpose of the stage and the effectiveness of the dramatic presentation will be seriously handicapped. Not only should the stage be of sufficient height above the main floor of the fellowship hall to permit good visibility but the stage lighting needs to receive special attention. The most important requisite in designing the wiring for the stage is to make provision for adequate electrical power supplied by a branch circuit that comes directly from the main distribution center. This branch should not supply other areas such as kitchens, pantry, classrooms, etc. The capacity of this supply will depend upon the size of stage and auditorium. Since the first cost between a hundred-ampere and a two-hundred-ampere supply is not excessive, it is recommended that the minimum should be two hundred amperes for either the three-wire single phase or the four-wire three phase system. This capacity may be in excess of what is required at the time the building is erected, but as the drama program grows and more power is required, this added capacity will be found necessary. It is much more economical to install it at the beginning than to try to adjust the system afterwards.

There should be a list of locations on the stage and over the auditorium where electrical outlets can be provided. The number of outlets given is for a minimum stage having an acting area of approximately 250 to 300 square feet.

1. Stage floor pockets. There should be a minimum of five having four separate twenty-ampere circuits

per pocket located, one down left, one down right, one up left, one up right, and one up center.

2. Teaser plugging strip. This is a sheet metal box or wire way approximately the same length as the proscenium opening hung immediately behind the cloth teaser referred to above. It should have ten twenty-ampere circuits with two outlets per circuit, and eight twenty-ampere circuits, four located on the left end of the strip, and four on the right end of the strip.

3. A second border plugging strip. Hang this six to eight feet upstage from the teaser plugging strip. The strip should have eight twenty-ampere circuits with two outlets per circuit.

4. Auditorium ceiling spotlight plugging strips. These are similar in construction to the teaser plugging strips. They should be installed over the auditorium social hall ceiling where space above permits easy access. Otherwise, they should be installed below the ceiling in a specially designed cove which harmonizes with the architectural features of the room. The cove should be large enough to mask the lights from the eyes of the audience and to provide easy access from the front and below for mounting and focusing the lights.

5. Footlight plugging pockets. Permanently connected disappearing footlights are a waste of money as footlights are not a primary source of illumination for the stage. Portable footlight strips may be used, when necessary, and plugged into the footlight plugging pockets, which are similar to the floor pockets. There should be two footlight plugging pockets, one at the front of the stage in the stage floor at the left, and one on the right. Each should contain three twenty-ampere circuits.

We emphasize again that none of the stage circuits listed above should be connected directly to the source of electrical power, but should terminate at a cross connecting panel, sometimes referred to as a patch panel. The lighting control system may consist of an arrangement of permanently installed autotransformers, or it may be a special switching panel designed to be used in conjunction with portable dimming equipment or with a permanently installed dimming control system, that may be added to the building sometime after the building has been completed. The only permanently connected lights on the stage should be the stage work lights.

Storage space for scenery, costumes, and property should be provided immediately adjacent to the stage. This will protect the equipment and save arduous labor and possible marring of the building where stage equipment has to be carried to and from a distant storage room.

In most instances, by careful planning, dressing rooms can be omitted and adjacent class or club rooms be adapted for dressing room and make-up purposes. Where the church can afford it, it is better, of course, to provide dressing rooms and toilet facilities in the immediate vicinity of the stage and as an integral part of the dramatics program of the church.

Central Staging

In recent years, so-called "central staging" or "theatre-in-the round" in which the audience is seated around the acting area, has become increasingly popular. The revival of this ancient procedure calls for a stage measuring approximately ten feet by fifteen feet, elevated only six inches above the floor, placed in the center of a large room. The audience is seated on all four sides. Scenery is practically uncalled for. Only a few stage props and furniture are used. A neutral or solid colored rug is placed over the stage floor area. Aisles for the actors, stage hands, and audience run diagonally from the four corners of the central stage. All audience seating is at floor level about the stage, if not more than four rows of seats are required, and placed in concentric rectangles around all four sides of the stage. Lighting is effected by the use of four spotlights placed above each of the four corners of the stage.

While the intimacy established between the audience and the actors, and the simplicity of the equipment required, together with the effectiveness of the dramatic procedure, indicate an increasing use of this method, churches should be warned that it is a false presumption to assume that this style of production is easier and less expensive to handle than the traditional proscenium open stage.

The closeness of the audience to the actors and the sparing use of scenery make it imperative that the costumes, properties, and the lighting be of the highest order. In a successful arena performance, the lighting is very largely depended upon to create the emotional interpretation of the play. The correct mounting of lighting instruments for these theatre-in-the-round programs is difficult. In order to provide as many lighting instruments as are required to light the acting area properly, it takes almost as much wiring installation as for the traditional stage.

The lighting instruments should be mounted in relation to the acting area in such a way that the angle of light reaches the stage at about 37 degrees to 45 degrees. The light source instruments will need to be mounted sufficiently high to keep them out of range of the eyes of the people in the audience. Inasmuch as there is no curtain which can be drawn at the end of each scene or act, or at the end of the play itself, good lighting control is even more important in this type of production than in the regular stage productions.

As previously indicated, when plays of this sort are given in a social hall, the church will need to provide portable platforms. These should be sufficiently rigid so the actors can move about on them freely without generating unnecessary noise. The height of the platform will depend upon the seating arrangement. It is felt best to limit the seating to about three rows surrounding the stage. The platform should be collapsible so it can be readily moved and stored.

Churches are well advised to procure the advice of a competent consultant, and also a person familiar with the dramatic requirements of a church when planning for the stage for dramatic productions. While this may incur some initial expense for the proper guidance, it will save the church, in the long run, from buying unnecessary equipment or installing items which are not geared to the dramatic requirements of the average church. The average sales engineer is not always competent to make the proper installations or to guide the church in the selection of the proper equipment.

The Kitchen

A well planned, well equipped kitchen is important, both as a place for useful work and for fellowship. The church kitchen needs to be carefully planned and equipped for use by volunteer help. For this reason, it will tend to be larger than the professional use, and will require more table and work space. The equipment should be of extra good quality to stand the hard usage and indifferent care to which it is usually subjected.

The kitchen usually requires floor space equal to about 20 per cent of the floor space of the parish or fellowship hall. Kitchen planning should provide for the orderly movement of food from its raw condition in storage through its preparation, the cooking and serving counters, and then for distribution either from the counter in cafeteria style or to the tables for more formal procedures. The dishwashing equipment should likewise be so placed that dirty dishes move readily from the receiving counter through the washing processes to storage without interfering with the preparation and distribution of the food in the kitchen.

The serving area, separated from the kitchen by a serving counter and from the fellowship hall by a set of double hung doors, will make it possible to keep all waitresses out of the kitchen and, at the same time, provide a double sound barrier between the kitchen and the parish hall so dishes may be washed at the same time a program is being carried forward in the hall itself.

The following illustrations show a small, medium, and large sized kitchens with suggestions as to the orderly movement of food from its raw state in storage to the tables in the dining room.[1]

In addition to the regular kitchen, which should be made available to all groups within the church, some churches find it necessary to provide auxiliary kitchenettes or pullman kitchens either opening into small social or club rooms, or so placed on a corridor that they can be readily opened and accessible for food distribution to small groups in nearby club or social rooms. Such installations require little space, and can be made readily accessible simply by opening a set of doors. They can likewise be concealed by closing the doors. These kitchenettes are most convenient and

spare the larger kitchen from being disarranged by small groups who only need cooking space for light refreshments.

Kitchen floor surfaces require grease- and waterproof, resilient, non-skid tile sloped to a drain. Walls, ceilings, and all woodwork should be finished with washable, high gloss enamel paint. A five-foot high wainscoating of porcelain tile around all walls is recommended. Acoustical tile or other porous or semi-porous wall and ceiling material should not be used.

A mechanical exhaust system is required to vent kitchen of cooking fumes. Outside light and ventilation are preferred. Windows should be screened. The kitchen should have a delivery entrance from outside for delivery of food and for garbage disposal.

Adequate storage cabinets equipped with labels and locks are also needed. Lighting outlets should provide fifty-foot candles of evenly distributed light for the kitchen area.

Storage Space

Accessible storage space for tables and chairs is essential for the variety of activities associated with the fellowship hall. A storage room with double hung, double doors to insure easy movement of chairs, tables, and trucks, with ample floor space, is preferred to under-stage storage. The latter is usually cramped and difficult of access.

Storage also needs to be provided immediately adjacent to the kitchen so reserve supplies of canned goods and other materials can be stored properly. Ample refrigeration will be required for larger churches where a great many meals are served, and where all the cooking is done in the church building.

As a matter of public health, it is very important that food should be prepared in the kitchen rather than carried from homes and kept for some time before serving. Increasingly, public officials are bearing down upon the necessity of strict sanitary precautions in church kitchens where meals are served to the public. The number of food poisoning cases originating in church dining facilities is making food processing a matter for greater attention on the part of present day churches.

Tables and Chairs

Churches should be warned against purchasing cheap, unsatisfactory tables and chairs. They are a poor investment. Tables should be sturdy, smooth finished, free from sharp or rough edges or braces, light weight, and equipped with good quality metal folding legs which assure solid bracing and easy manipulation.

Good quality, sturdily built metal folding chairs designed for good posture and comfort, are preferred to the nonfolding type. The former store in less space, are less subjected to breakage and marring, and are more readily transported to other parts of the building when needed.

KITCHEN[1]

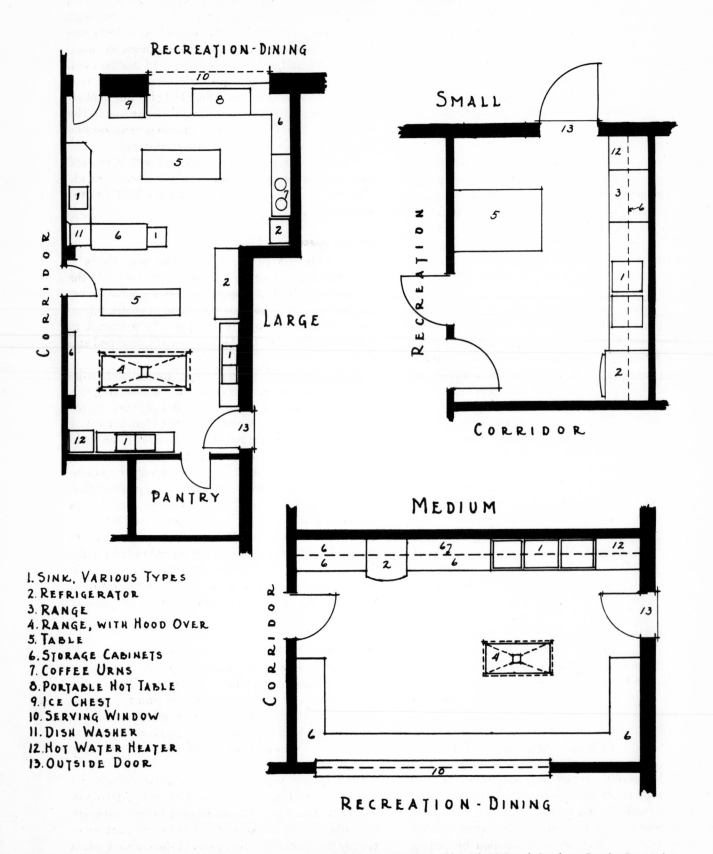

RECREATION-DINING

CORRIDOR

LARGE

PANTRY

SMALL

RECREATION

CORRIDOR

MEDIUM

CORRIDOR

RECREATION-DINING

1. SINK, VARIOUS TYPES
2. REFRIGERATOR
3. RANGE
4. RANGE, WITH HOOD OVER
5. TABLE
6. STORAGE CABINETS
7. COFFEE URNS
8. PORTABLE HOT TABLE
9. ICE CHEST
10. SERVING WINDOW
11. DISH WASHER
12. HOT WATER HEATER
13. OUTSIDE DOOR

1 *Manual of Church Building Standards* Department of Church Architecture, Baptist Sunday School Board, Southern Baptist Convention

Rubber tired metal trucks should be provided for transporting tables and chairs from storage, as required.

Generally Speaking

The parish hall, where no other room is available, can be readily made attractive for wedding receptions and other similar events in the church life. Two or three large colorful floor rugs can be placed on the parish hall floor immediately in front of the stage area. One or two attractive floor lamps can be placed to give this area a homelike atmosphere. A table spread with a suitable cloth and decorated with candlesticks will serve as a place for light refreshments. This particular end of the room can readily be screened with attractive portable screens so as to reduce the large floor area to more intimate proportions. If the church is fortunate enough to have a few pieces of colorful occasional furniture, these will add to the homelike atmosphere of the parish hall when used for these more intimate and smaller fellowships.

Where a special recreation or "rumpus" room is not available, we suggest that tables for ping pong and other group games be provided, and provision be made in the storage room for their reception when not in use. It will also be wise to have a number of sturdily built tables, approximately of the dimension of "card" tables. These can be set up for table games or put together in groups to form one long table for a small luncheon. Several of the furniture manufacturing companies build these tables much stronger than the standard card table, and thereby make them adequate for many diversified uses for small fellowship occasions.

See "Use Dramatics in Your Church," "Basic Requirements for Church Dramatics," and "Lighting the Church Stage," all by Arthur S. Risser. These reprints available from the National Council of Churches, Office of Publication and Distribution, 120 E. 23rd Street, New York 10, N. Y. Price 10c each.

CHAPTER 16

Improving What You Have..

This chapter is addressed to those church school leaders who must, for a number of reasons, use existing buildings which, while the worse for wear, can be greatly improved without drastic alterations or lavish outlays of money. The suggestions which follow look to the improvement of these buildings, and deal mainly with the most fundamental considerations.

Cleanliness

The simplest and smallest, as well as the most pretentious buildings can be made attractive and beautiful by cleanliness and good housekeeping. These things are fundamental. They will not happen of themselves: they need to be planned for, and some person or persons must sense their importance, and bring them into existence. They have a very definite bearing upon the teaching and ministry of the Christian Church.

Look around your building with a critical eye. Perhaps you have become accustomed to it and do not sense that through neglect and poor housekeeping it has fallen into a sorry state. It is all too common to find that church buildings are so dirty and ill-kept as to make them depressing and forbidding. Such conditions as we have observed in churches across the country might, with charity, be forgiven in some of the backward countries of the world. But what excuse have we to offer for dirt and disorder in classrooms, storage areas cluttered with odds and ends of useless material. Even the sanctuaries of our edifices are far from savory and wholesome. Often floors, windows, walls, woodwork, draperies, furniture, and carpets show lack of even the most ordinary care. Floors and the corners of rooms are coated with layers of dirt and impregnated wax. Paint has been allowed to wear off, and the dirt has been ground into the floor surfaces so as to make them forbidding, if not unsanitary.

Frequently we find that church kitchens, used not only for the preparation of food, but for classrooms for children, are nauseating because they have not been properly ventilated. The old coffee grounds, flower stalks, paper towels, and bits of garbage left in the container add their quota to the depressing conditions of walls and floors and woodwork in general.

Without taking offense at these critical appraisals, become a little child for a moment. Imagine what the effect upon a sensitive youngster must be when he is led into such surroundings. It would not be difficult to imagine a child forming, perhaps unconsciously, a positive dislike for all that is associated with the church building. We know of adults who have been inhibited in their religious life by less disturbing elements than those already mentioned. It would not be remiss to state that cleanliness in the House of God is a part of the technique of Christian education and evangelism. Visit the rest rooms in your church buildings. Are they clean and sanitary even though very inadequately equipped? Soap, water, paint, and a good disinfecting fluid will work miracles in such places, and make them less offensive to people of normal cleanliness. The poorest church can afford these essentials.

Order and Beauty

To a considerable extent, the appearance of the church school building, both from the exterior and the interior, reveals the degree of concern with which a church views its sacred ministry. This is not intended to be an accusation or a reflection, but a simple statement of the fact that people are impressed by the outer as well as the inner events that transpire within a given building.

To the unsympathetic and casual observer, many church buildings are, apparently, dedicated to a god called "Clutter." Seemingly, much of the bric-a-brac discarded by successive generations gravitates to the interior of our church buildings. Valuable space is thereby pre-empted, and the church takes over the prerogatives of a public museum. Unused literature of uncertain value, bedraggled posters and banners, unsightly pictures hung awry, tattered hymnbooks left lying around, odds and ends of neglected wearing apparel, chairs and tables in bad repair, scarred woodwork, stained walls—such things do injustice to the very significant ministry the church is called upon to perform. They are all matters which can be readily remedied. It is difficult to believe that a church which really means business will permit such clutter and ugliness within its building.

At times, we need to be brave enough to clear out all materials not definitely related to the work of the church, and particularly to the furtherance of the teaching procedures. Supplies and accessories should be stored in convenient, suitable places. This will permit them to be kept clean and classified so they may be quickly found and used. Even open shelving will permit the sorting and classifying of Sunday school materials and placing an identifying label on the front of the shelf, thereby rendering a service to the church school, and effecting economies in conserving literature.

Again, we emphasize that large expenditures of money are seldom necessary to effect striking improvements in many church school buildings. Some of the brightest, neatest, and most attractive classrooms are found in the buildings of churches of modest income. Neatness, cleanliness, the exercise of good taste, clean windows, appropriate shades and draperies, a few good religious pictures, a vase of flowers, well kept walls and woodwork finished in quiet but cheerful colors, add much to the beauty and charm of any room.

Let us not forget that for some people the time spent in a church school building is the only inkling they have of the beauty of God and of his great love and thoughtfulness. Those who have good homes and pleasant surroundings for their daily work should not be invited to lower their standards when they come within the church edifice. Others, not so fortunate, should at least have some intimations of that order of truth, beauty, and goodness for which the church stands.

Heat and Ventilation

In his article, "The Seven Deadly Sins of Church Architecture,"[1] Halford E. Luccock names bad air as one of the chief enemies of the learning process. "Bad air—carbon dioxide—is a deadly drug which deadens the brain. Now in the conduct of worship (he might well have said 'teaching') there abideth three things, art, music, air, but the greatest of these is air." Good fresh air and pupil attention and interest are closely related. Surely a church committee administering the property will be glad to see that the Sunday school areas are properly aired before use on Sunday or weekday activities. Not infrequently, the foul air from the previous Sunday is reheated and recirculated. Little wonder people complain of "that church smell." Little wonder pupils are restless, drowsy, irritable, and inattentive. Teaching cannot go well in such an environment; pupils do not carry away with them either the subject shared or a pleasant impression of the hours spent in the church under such conditions.

In some instances, church rooms are heated by individual heating units which draw upon the air within the room for the oxygen necessary for combustion. Imagine twenty children being crowded into one of these rooms already seriously depleted of oxygen. Such things happen. Consider, if you will, the danger to the health of children when epidemics of colds and children's diseases are making their rounds. Such a classroom is a menace to the health of the community. Think, too, of the absenteeism due to sickness induced by such surroundings.

While we do not recommend putting in transoms over doorways entering the hallways for the reason that sound is conveyed to the room to the distraction of teachers and pupils, these are to be preferred to lack of fresh air within the classrooms.

Windows can be carefully designed with deflectors to prevent direct drafts upon pupils. Fresh air ducts made of fire resisting materials and inexpensively constructed can be used with a fan system to circulate fresh air and to withdraw the stale air from classroom areas. At least, those in charge can see to it that all rooms are thoroughly aired immediately before and after use. Incidentally, fresh air heats and circulates much more readily than foul air, and has an important bearing upon the consumption of fuel.

Adequate heating is another important aid to good teaching. Pupils required to sit in cold, damp rooms are never in the best frame of mind to give keen attention even to the best of teaching. Cold feet have been known to retard many persons where high adventure was pending. Overheating is also detrimental to the health and the attention of persons enclosed within a classroom. Occasionally, a heating system, for want of minor repairs, gives off copious amounts of smoke or coal gas. This is not good for persons who have to breathe the air thus contaminated, but it also materially increases the cost of re-decorating walls thus soiled and disfigured. Occasionally, we find a well intentioned church caretaker who is an accessory before and after the fact by virtue of his having closed off the ducts which would permit the cold but clean fresh air to enter the heat-circulating system or to get into the buildings. He acts on the theory that the cold air thus allowed into the building makes it more difficult to heat, and runs up the fuel bill. It should be remembered that just heating it does not put oxygen into the air, nor does it take out the carbon dioxide given off by the human body. Clean, fresh air with proper regulation of temperature are essential in a building used for Christian education.

Seating

Public school teachers and psychologists have long emphasized the direct relation between physical posture and mental attitudes. Correct posture is conducive to both physical well-being and mental alertness. A slovenly, lounging position induces indifferent attention. Ill fitting chairs are the cause of much difficulty, especially where small children are concerned.

It is poor economy, indeed, to buy cheap chairs, or to bequeath to defenseless children old chairs or secondhand benches that are not designed for child use. Church committees will be well repaid for giving careful consideration to the seating to be installed in the several rooms and departments of their educational building. A good chair should provide a well shaped support in the small of the pupil's back just above the hips. The seat must not be too long from front to back, and should slope backwards so the pupil's weight keeps him against the back of the chair in an erect and alert position. Seats should be correct in height so the pupil's feet can rest firmly upon the floor without pressure from the front edge of the seat against the pupil's legs. Such pressure on the backs of the legs inhibits the circulation of blood, and causes great discomfort. Pupils cannot give attention when they are made uncomfortable by such conditions.

Chairs for pupils up to the primary department should have no sharp corners, should be rounded off and smooth, and treated to resist heat and moisture. Chairs should also be stained or treated to blend into the color scheme of the particular room or department. Avoid strong and variegated colors in the chairs and tables within the classroom.

Tables

Good tables for class use should be made of good wood, and should be kept in good repair. Stretchers should not be permitted to interfere with the child's legs or to damage his person or clothing. Recommended chair and table heights are set forth in the chapters dealing with the needs of preschool, elementary school, and youth groups.

The "U" shaped and kidney tables in vogue in times past are not recommended.

Light and Color

Many classrooms are unnecessarily dark and uninviting because the window glass is either dirty or so deeply colored with needless and sometimes offensive cheap colored glass as to shut out the daylight. A study of one city church showed that the heavily frosted window glass was less than 50 per cent efficient in letting in the outside light because of dirt adhering to the outside of the glass. These windows had not been washed on the outside for many years. Clear glass is to be recommended in preference to the so-called "ecclesiastical" glass frequently used years ago in church school buildings.

Proper lighting is very definitely an important aid to successful teaching. Eye strain caused either by too intense light from fixtures or windows, or lack of illumination, does a grave disservice to the pupils, and contributes to inattention and poor discipline. Pupils should never be called upon to face directly into the source of light.

Where artificial light is required, make sure that the light bulbs are not directly in evidence. There are many inexpensive fixtures on the market, and any church can afford to correct faulty lighting.

Attention should be given to the light-reflecting qualities of wall coverings. A dark green surface, which for some reason is frequently used in church school buildings, absorbs some 60 per cent of all light shining upon it. On the other hand, a white surfaced wall will reflect approximately 70 per cent of light impinging upon it. Naturally, classrooms for children or youth should not be finished in cold, stark white. Walls are the background for the furnishings of the room, and give character to the teaching environment. They can be made attractive, inviting, and yet inconspicuous by the use of soft, mellow color tones. Strong colors, especially red, bright blue, and bright yellow, should be avoided. Wall surfaces should be finished smooth so they will paint well, and to eliminate pores where dust collects.

Light and color should be studied together. If you increase the intensity of the light, you change the color factor. Or, again, if you intensify the color factor, you modify the intensity of the light. It should be remembered that the same color will vary greatly in different rooms. Colors should be chosen in view of the natural light, the nature of the wall surface, the way the paint is to be applied.

Persons inexperienced in the use of color, will be well advised to procure the services either of a color expert or of a competent architect. Color, wisely handled, can do wonderful things to the appearance of a room. Few amateurs are qualified to decorate the walls of a church school building. The color scheme for the whole church school building should be planned as a whole, and the details for each room should be carefully considered. (See Chapter VI.)

Sound Control

Many of our older buildings were erected in days when little attention was given to the control of sound. In other instances, rooms which were well designed from that point of view have been made less effective by the use of high gloss paint and other materials which have closed up the pores in the wall texture, and have made the ceilings, walls, and floors so hard finished as to make them excellent media for reverberating sound within a given room. These conditions can be improved by the use of a sound-absorbing material on the ceiling, by careful placing of window draperies and, where usage permits, a soft carpet on the floor. So much for sound which is generated within the given room.

Sound also comes from outside the classroom, and either comes through the partitions and floors which are not built substantially enough or properly designed to control sound, or disturbing noises may come through doors or the spaces under the doors or around the heating system or through heating ducts or other media which are so arranged as to lend themselves to transferring sound from other parts of the building. Where the latter conditions obtain, the church would be well advised to procure the services of a competent architect or acoustical engineer. The cost for such professional service will be amply repaid in the improved conditions which can be effected by their suggestions.

General Furnishings for Classrooms and Assemblies

Much of what has been said in previous chapters will apply to the refurbishing of an old building. The church would be well advised to study the total building and to itemize, after careful investigation, the particular improvements which can be made in a given area, and also to set out in detail the items of furniture which should be dispensed with, and the furnishings which should be procured. The same consideration should be given to the floors, walls, ceilings, and windows.

In most instances, it will not be possible to effect all

the needed changes at once, but if a program is carefully detailed and the available funds budgeted across a period of time, ultimately the desired results can be effected.

Music

Music is important in the religious training of children. Musical instruments should be kept in tune and, when not to be used, should be locked to protect them from misuse. It certainly is not to the glory of God nor to the honest training of children to have hymns played off key on a piano that emits uncertain sounds. If the old pianos or reed organs in your church are out of tune, see to it that they are properly tuned. If they are not in good enough condition to warrant such expenditures, have them taken out of the building so the floor space can be used to advantage. The day when "anything will do for the church" has gone. Christian education is no longer a secondary affair.

Do It Yourself

Modern materials and the "do-it-yourself" techniques make possible the refurbishing of rooms and equipment by the wise use of a well directed and carefully organized volunteer service by members of the church parish. Not too many persons are qualified to select color schemes and to do the finer carpentry work. Be sure to enlist competent direction for the planning and for the more technical undertakings, and organize your volunteer workers to carry out, under competent direction, the types of work which can be done by amateurs.

A careful organization and supervision of workers is essential for volunteer projects. In order to sustain interest and to get any appreciable amount of work accomplished, it will be necessary to have all materials and tools carefully prepared and laid out, and all preliminary preparations made, and definite assignment of each person to a particular piece of work. Publicizing each completed project encourages the workers, increases the general support of the church in the project, and is always an inducement to undertake other improvements of a similar nature.

The great variety of new materials such as plastic fabrics, plywood panels, and wall boards can be used to cover unsightly wall surfaces. Acoustical tile for rooms with too much reverberation, attractive floor coverings which can be laid by amateurs, can be used to refurbish unsightly basement rooms, and to make rooms above grade cheerful and attractive.

The fellowship engendered, the interest created, and the understanding of the purpose of the Christian Church arising out of these well organized volunteer projects exemplifies religious education at its best, and renders a very worth-while service to the cause for which the church stands in the community.

CHAPTER 17

Meeting the Needs of the Small Church......

Let it be said emphatically that the small church is usually small only in the numbers of persons involved, the limitations of its resources, space, equipment, and leadership. Certainly it is not small in the importance of its contribution to Christian leadership as a roll call of the outstanding persons of any generation will attest.

True, the small church is frequently confronted with many handicaps. These are not insurmountable. Courage, imagination, an appraisal of resources, patience, and willingness to experiment, and a high sense of Christian dedication can work wonders in the least promising situations.

The suggestions offered in this chapter are by way of encouragement, and by no means exhaust the possibilities for improving the teaching ministry of smaller congregations.

Taking Stock

First, determine by actual count, the number of persons and their ages, which fall within the church's area of responsibility. Then decide, in the light of what has been said in Chapters V, VII-X, about grouping and grading, how your particular church school can be organized to provide possible learning experiences within the limited space you have available. Approximate the ideal standards in so far as your best efforts and the limitations of space permit. It is usually better to have sizable groups with a wider age span with good leadership than to have too many small classes. Appraise your building and equipment after again reading Chapter XVI. Discover and list in detail the items of furniture which should be removed for the reason that they now serve no useful purpose and occupy needless space which you propose to adapt to better teaching procedures.

Carefully study the space you have. If it is a one-room edifice, you may well consider which areas will be suited to the needs of each of the groups. Perhaps you can take out some of the pews if they are not needed regularly and thus get some floor space at the rear corners of the room which will permit attractive arrangement of children's classes and materials. In some instances, pews at the front and rear of the church are not fastened permanently to the floor. These can be turned about and spaced to permit a class to face inward toward a wall and the teacher, and thereby give a measure of protection from distraction and at the same time afford a sense of group solidarity.

Lapboards, made of masonite or some other smooth hard surfaced thin board, can be readily made for each pupil. These can rest on the pupil's knees and will provide a suitable working surface for writing and drawing.

Corners of the one-room church next to the pulpit can sometimes be enclosed by attractive portable

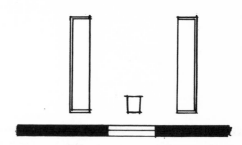

No. 1 affords the simplest arrangement. A small table of approximately card table size with a chair can be placed in the enclosed area.

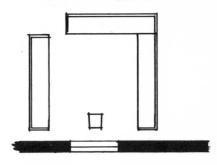

No. 2 illustrates another arrangement of pews which can be made along a wall. The attention of the pupils is focused toward the wall and away from distractions within the room.

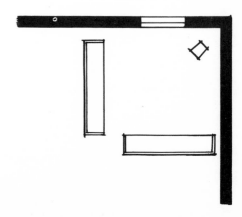

No. 3 shows use of a corner area with pupils facing inward. Portable storage cabinets of the homemade variety will permit ready arrangement of these pews areas for teaching. See page 82.

screens. See Scheme IV. These screens not only mitigate against distraction emanating from other classes but afford surfaces for pinning up pictures, posters, and other items of interest. Screens can be constructed as a single panel to provide a straight wall surface, in two panel sections with hinges to be used as a corner wall, or in three panel sections with hinges to make possible a combination of wall shapes.

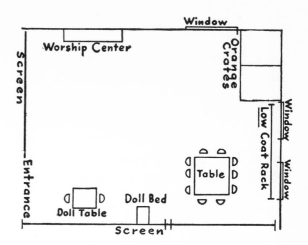

Corner in a Small Church

Here, a corner of a room, perhaps in the kitchen or in front of the place of worship of a one-room church building, is screened off so the children have a place of their own.

Pictures are hung at eye level on the attractive screen; the homemade furniture is painted in a contrasting color (not gaudy). A simple drapery is hung back of a low table to provide an informal center of religious interest for the age group concerned.

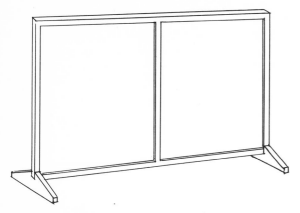

Portable Screen Mounted on Casters

Panels can be treated to serve as chalkboards, pin-up areas for pictures and hand work. These screens can be moved readily and stored out of the way when not needed.

Three Panel Screen

The sections of this screen are fastened together with hinges. They can be folded for storage or when open used in various ways to enclose space for teaching purposes.

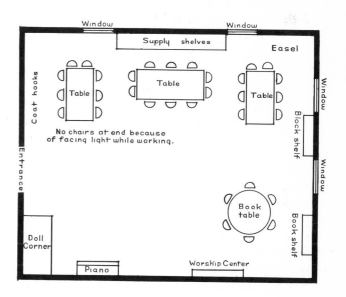

1. Drop-leaf table fastened on back of pew.

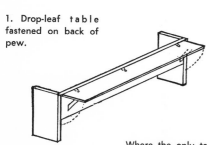

2. Drop-leaf table fastened to the wall.

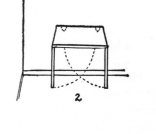

Where the only teaching space available is the place of worship the above are indications of provisions which can be made for needed table space. Drawing No. 1 shows a hinged shelve on the back of a few. Drawing No. 2 shows a hinged shelf attached to a wall.

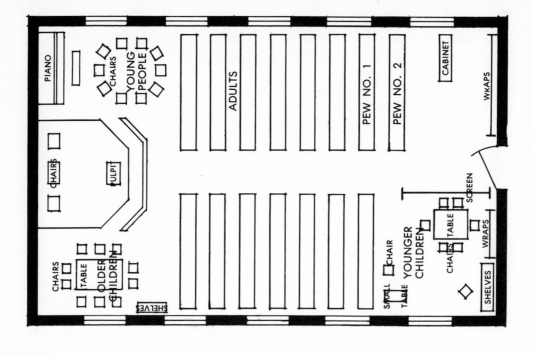

No. VIII. Another possible arrangement of a one-room church.[2]

Pew No. 1 can be turned around and pew No. 2 can be pulled back to permit use of a small class.

See Figures Nos. I and III, Page 121 of this chapter.

1—KINDERGARTEN

1. Supply cabinet
2. Folding table
3. Book rack screen
4. Display cabinet
5. Stools
6. Doll's bed
7. Easel for painting
8. Paper rack
9. Wall bag for small articles
10. Box for small treasures
11. Water for washing hands
12. Chairs
13. Pew used as table

2—PRIMARY GROUP

14. Partitioned box for supplies
15. Supply cabinets
16. Table top placed on supply cabinets
17. Screen—also as bulletin board
18. Pads for sitting on floor
19. Pews used for seating and picture display
20. Nail kegs for chairs

3—JUNIOR GROUP

21. Supply cabinet table
22. Supply cabinets (2)
23. Narrow table top placed on supply cabinets
24. Chart rack
25. Lapboards
26. Pews for seating
27. Teacher's chair

No. VII. Possible arrangement of a one-room church edifice.

(See "How to Make Church School Equipment," Adair and McCort, pages 10 and 11 for suggestions.[1])

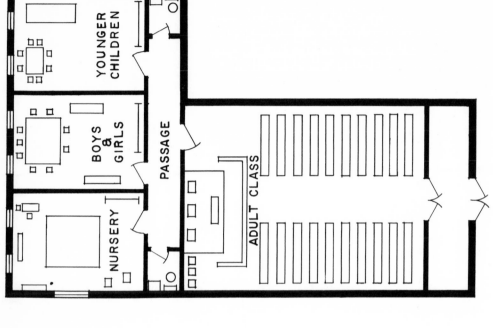

No. X. Arrangement where three rooms and more are available.

No. IX. A possible arrangement for a large basement or fellowship hall when classrooms are not available.[3]

Youth and adults use the place of worship for their classes.

No. XI. Storage Cabinet.

Combination Cabinet and Table

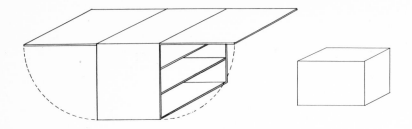

Open for use as a table   Closed during church service   Simple Homemade storage Cabinet

Improvising

Where you have more than one room—one or two rooms opening off the place of worship or a large open basement room—you may well consider some of the following possibilities:

1. Make certain that the available rooms are assigned to the groups who both by average attendance and the greatest need should be using them.

2. Study possible changes in program scheduling which will permit different groups to use these spaces at different times.

3. If one room is a kitchen, study the possibility of so arranging and enclosing the kitchen equipment in homemade cabinets that space can be conserved and made more pleasing for class use. A table or tables can have adjustable legs so they can be lowered to the proper height for use by the children. Folding chairs of proper height for the age group should also be provided. Church school cabinets mounted on casters which can be readily moved when the kitchen is needed for its regular use can be made by home talent.

Portable storage cabinet mounted on casters

Description of materials of construction
    3 pieces 1″ x 10″, x the length of the shelves desired
    1 piece 1″ x 10″, x 2″ longer than these 3 pieces
    2 pieces 1″ x 10″, x the height desired
    4 10″ lengths of quarter round to use as shelf supports
    2 10″ lengths of 2″ x 4″s for bottom supports for casters
    4 casters
    4 corner brackets for reinforcing each corner at the back
     Finishing nails
For younger children the back of such a cabinet can be covered with wallboard to be used as a place to display pictures, etc.

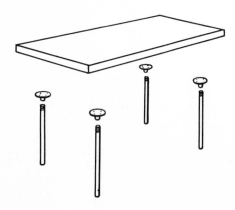

Screw pipe flanges (a) to bottom of table; screw threaded pipe legs (b) into flanges.
By use of different length legs, table height can be adjusted for each age group.

(See "How To Make Church School Equipment," Adair and McCort, page 32, for suggestions on No. XIV and page 33 for No. XV.)[4]

4. The following suggestions are offered for use of a building with a large room other than the place of worship:

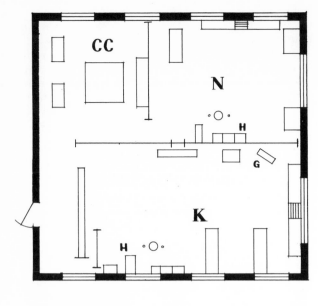

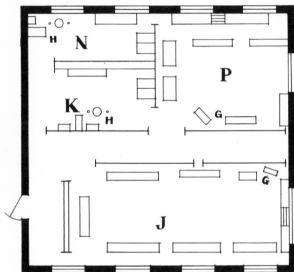

10:00-12:00 A.M.   NURSERY AND KINDERGARTEN:

(In basement during church service)
Under three years in kitchen; 3's in Room II; 4's
and 5's in Room I

Scheme (a)

CC = Care center-cribs, play pen cupboards
 N = Nursery—Washable rugs on floor, cupboards, tables, cup-
boards, a few chairs
 K = Kindergarten—much same as nursery
Portable screens and coat
racks should be numbered
so they can be easily
placed for each Sunday's use
 H = Housekeeping center
 G = Worship center (informal)
 J = Juniors

Scheme (b)

This scheme shows same space divided differently to include juniors.
Furnishings similar to (a) above.

—tables (if in open room or at right angle to wall)

—cupboards and shelves (if against wall)

Room planned for all children's groups.

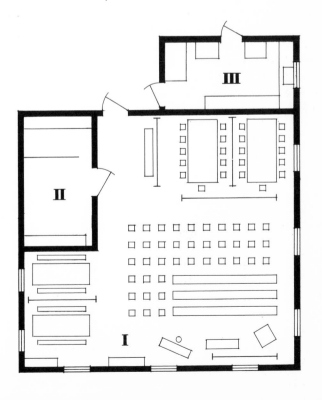

Scheme (c) which we outline below, envisions a
multiple use of space, a practice which is becoming
increasingly in evidence in church school endeavors:

See "How To Make Church School Equipment,"
Adair and McCort, page 35 for suggestions.

Scheme (c)

Schedule Example with Corresponding Use of Rooms in Scheme (c)
above:

9:00- 9:50 A.M.   PRIMARY DEPARTMENT:

Rooms I, II, III (in basement); largest department
with average attendance of 60; six classes

10:00-10:50 A.M.   JUNIORS:

Rooms I, II
JUNIOR HIGHS:
In sanctuary; seniors joined for worship
SENIOR HIGHS:
In room III, spilling over into furnace room
ADULTS:
In pastor's study

Adjustable tables previously illustrated are used except in the kitchen. Portable screens divide the space and are numbered to go into same places each week.

Room II is equipped with shelves for library and equipment for the school.

For further amplification of the possibilities of space and equipment use in the small church, we refer you to *How to Make Church School Equipment,* Thelma Adair and Elizabeth McCort, Westminster Press. With permission of the publishers, we have quoted freely from this excellent manual.

Using Audio-Visuals

Effective use can be made of limited equipment under what may seem impossible conditions. In his article, "The Small Church Can Use Audio-Visuals in Its Classes," Virgil E. Foster[5] tells us how it can be done. "Let us presume," says he, "that the most difficult situation—a one-room church, with clear or nearly clear windows, which let in much sunlight, with about six classes in the pews and corners, separated by only five or six feet. Or a department with several classes meeting in the same room. Even under these conditions audio-visuals can be used." He then offers the following constructive suggestions which we summarize:

1. Use one or more simple slide viewers costing $1.95-$3.00, into which slides can be inserted. These will magnify slides and some of them will take filmstrips. They can be passed from pupil to pupil in the class.

2. Use a nonmagnifying viewer consisting of opaque glass placed over the open end of a small box into which small electric bulbs have been placed. Slides can be laid on the glass and viewed with a magnifying glass.

3. Use electric magnifying viewers available in a wide variety of models in prices ranging from $5.00 to $25.00.

4. Use a large viewer which projects the slide from the rear by use of a mirror onto a small screen. A small group of eight to twelve pupils can see all details of the picture thus projected. Cost, $37.50 to $97.50.

5. Use an ordinary cardboard box about fifteen inches by fifteen inches square; cut two square ten inch by ten inch holes on opposite sides; glue a square of architect's tracing cloth over one opening. Use a slide or filmstrip projector to project the picture through the box onto the tracing cloth which is placed to face the pupils. Slides will need to be reversed horizontally from the usual procedure.

6. Use a regular screen but place the projector within four or five feet of the screen. This gives a reasonably bright picture, if care is taken to have the least possible window light fall upon the screen. Two small opaque side screens with a canopy over them placed in front of the viewing screen will serve to control side lighting interference.

7. Turn the screen away from other classes so it does not distract them. This may be done by using rear pews in a one room church.

8. Eliminate recorded narrative when using filmstrip and read the script in a modulated voice to avoid disturbing nearby classes.

9. Always seek to adjust use of audio-visual to the classes rather than classes to the equipment.

It is hoped that churches will strive to conform to the standards set forth in Chapter XII.

All that has been said in previous chapters concerning heating, ventilation, lighting, floor colors and decoration, applies in the small church as well as in the large.

It is hoped that the one-room church will not have to remain so for long. In many situations, greater concern for the interests of Christian education and a more worthy stewardship will make possible something far better than the minimum space and equipment. With the aid of competent architectural advice, many of our small church buildings can be remodeled or added to with comparatively small cost. New parishes should use such service in selecting their site and in planning the building program to permit building in units as the need for space grows and funds are available.

The important thing is to list your needed possible improvements, lay out a program of successive steps looking to its fulfillment, enlist the help of interested people, begin at the beginning and follow through step by step. One project successfully completed stimulates enthusiasm and evokes skills and resources in other persons.

---

[1] Reprinted from *How to Make Church School Equipment* by Adair and McCort, Copyright, 1955, by W. L. Jenkins, The Westminster Press. Used by permission.

[2] Emma Jane Kramer, *Equipment and Arrangement for Children's Groups in the Church*

[3] Ibid.

[4] See 1

[5] Virgil E. Foster, "The Small Church Can Use Audio-Visuals in its Classes," *International Journal of Religious Education,* (December, 1953)

—*How a Small Church Can Have Good Christian Education.* New York: Harper & Bros. 1955. See Chapter xi.

CHAPTER 18

Architectural Service

The choice of a competent architect is one of the most important steps in the building program. The wrong choice usually leads to a course of events and ultimate results that are unsatisfactory.

Avoid stock plans whether put out by the local lumber yard, common contractors, or cut-rate fee architects. Each church should be planned from the inside out to meet the particular requirements of each individual congregation. Seldom, if ever, do two churches need exactly the same size building and the same arrangement of floor space.

There are plenty of competent church architects. Make certain that you get the best. Expect to pay for such service. Thereby, you will save money in the long run and will save your church from living for generations with a building that is an architectural monstrosity and inefficient from the point of view of rendering Christian service.

Church planning is the most complex and difficult of all architectural problems. Within one structure, there must be a sanctuary for divine worship; a church school building, including rooms for training and worship; fellowship and recreation; plus rooms for administration and service. These parts—from the construction and design standpoint—are quite different, but in successful church work it is necessary to have these planned as one structure with a harmonious exterior design for the whole. This presents an intricate problem for the designing architect.

It is very important—especially in the field of Christian education—to procure the services of an architect who has kept himself abreast of the recent changes in educational procedures within the Christian Church.

At times, the church may—to its distinct advantage—engage the services of a consulting architect who plans the building and outlines its general design. He takes full responsibility for the architectural service rendered. He usually makes arrangements with a local architectural firm to supervise and administer the erection of the building. The fee charged is usually the standard one for that particular locality, and is divided on a basis mutually agreed upon by the architects concerned.

Selecting the Architect

Architecture is one of the learned professions. The competent architect must have technical skill and knowledge, business and executive ability, and an artistic sense, with a background of general scholarship.

His training includes courses in liberal arts, literature, and history as well as technical training in business administration, design, architecture, engineering, and purchasing. In addition, the designer of the House of God must have a deep awareness and understanding of the objectives of Christian education and the whole church program.

In most states, legal requirements include the examination and registration of practicing architects and forbid the use of the term, "architect," except by those licensed to practice in their jurisdiction. This is for the protection of those engaging architectural service.

The architect selected should be independent of the contractor and detached from any possible financial benefit to himself which might accrue to him through agreements with contractors or suppliers of goods or services to the job in hand.

Choose your architect thoughtfully. Training and ability are important. Worth considering, too, is personality. Remember that you are going to spend a great deal of your time with him. He is going to be closely associated with you in the developing of ideas and in the spending of thousands of dollars. What you can get in planning, good construction, low maintenance cost, and aesthetic appeal will depend upon the judgment and ability of the man you select and upon his willingness to work patiently with your committee.

Do not be carried away by pretty pictures. Any architect can have these drawn by a clever artist. Look for good, sound, practical planning.

Don't select an architect because his fees are less than those of his competitors. Minimum fees are prescribed by the American Institute of Architects. For this reason, the best architects can usually be procured at no greater cost than the poorest.

Find out from his past clients what they think of the architect and his work. They can give you some helpful information as to how efficiently he conducts his business.

Do not expect your architect to be a magician and pull a proverbial rabbit out of a hat. He can only function as far as you will permit him. He is a man trained in planning and designing. Give him a chance to show what he can do. A well conceived plan will almost invariably produce a good exterior.

You would do well to inquire as to whether the church architect you are considering is a churchman. As a churchman, he will sense what the church stands for and will be willing to bring to his work and approach an attitude which is truly religious rather than purely mechanical and personal. From your own denominational headquarters, or from the Bureau of Church Building of the National Council of Churches, you may secure a list of architects in your locality who have demonstrated their interest and aptitude for church design.

Architects' Fees

Expect to pay the architect a fair and reasonable fee. This fee must cover a wide range and variety of expenses. In addition to compensation for the service of the architect, you must understand that he has to pay draftsmen and engineers—the majority of whom are college trained people. He must also maintain an office force, take care of the rent and overhead expenses of his office, provide the necessary tools and supplies for preparing plans and blueprinting drawings, and also bear the cost of printing the specifications which set forth in detail the materials to be put into the building.

Generally speaking, the minimum fee the church should expect to pay for architectural service on a new building ranges from 7 to 8 per cent of the cost of the building plus any furnishing and equipment that are selected and installed under the architect's supervision. Remodeling undertakings demand a larger percentage due to the complexity of the operation and the time consumed in perfecting changes in older structures.

As a general rule—because of the complexity of the work—fees for church architectural service run slightly higher than those paid for commercial work.

The church building committee is well advised to secure a copy of the American Institute of Architects' standard form of contract. This will define, in general terms, the types of service rendered by the architect and will indicate the fees and percentages to be paid at each stage of the architect's program of planning.

Remodeling Existing Buildings

Great caution should be exercised in determining whether the building is worth the expenditure of large sums of money in remodeling. Remodeling jobs usually run much higher than the estimated cost due to the uncertainties confronting the architect and the builder in dealing with the problems in hand.

Due to the changes in the cost of labor in recent years, in many instances it has been found more economical to demolish the existing structure and erect a new building in its place. Frequently the old building when remodeled proves to be very costly and does not provide the facilities required by the church.

The program of remodeling should be approached with the same careful study as that given to a new structure.

(1) The church should survey its constituency to make certain that the church has a future ministry in its present location and that the contemplated expenditures are warranted and will produce a building adequate for the program requirements of the forseeable future.

(2) The church should complete a statement of space requirements room by room and age group by age group.

(3) The church should make a study of the existing building with the assistance of a competent architect or engineer to determine its structural adequacy and the feasibility of remodeling it. Such a study should have in mind the long run maintenance, cost, and serviceability of the building in the face of the changing needs of the modern world.

(4) The church should procure competent architectural service to plan the preliminary drawings and determine thereby the adequacy of the building and the probable cost for such remodeling.

(5) Remodeling plans, where it is found feasible, can be outlined so as to be built in units. Each unit can be cared for progressively as funds are available.

CHAPTER 19

Financing the Building Program......................................

Church people will give sacrificially to a worthy building campaign. However, they must be informed, inspired, organized, enlisted, and provided with a schedule of payments which will permit each, according to his ability, to fit into the total requirement.

Each church will be well advised to consult with the denominational leaders concerning financial requirements. Some denominations provide fund-raising service. Where such service is not provided advice will, undoubtedly, be forthcoming as to where good professional leadership may be procured. Fortunately for our churches the number of qualified leaders in this field has greatly increased in recent years and their techniques have produced more satisfactory results.

Experience and competent guidance in church building finance is essential to success. Haphazard or indifferent approaches to fund raising usually mean that a great deal of money is never procured and the whole building program suffers as a consequence.

There are no magic methods for raising money. The success of a financial campaign will largely depend upon the thoroughness with which the congregation is prepared both from the point of view of information and as to the religious significance of the undertaking.

If you plan to raise a substantial sum of money for building purposes, you would be well advised to procure outside leadership either from your denominational headquarters or from the several reliable firms now specializing in this important service. These trained people have the "know how" and usually raise sums far in excess of what local leadership can hope to achieve.

Make certain that the outside fund-raising leadership you employ trains and uses your own members to solicit the building funds. This is important and will have a lasting effect upon the Christian stewardship, outlook, and capacity of your congregation for years to come.

Be thorough in the preparation and promotion of your fund-raising efforts. Be sure to enlist every single individual before approaching organizations within the church or soliciting memorial gifts.

Present day experience indicates that successful campaigns do not extend for over a period of more than three years and are usually based on weekly or monthly payments.

While large gifts are important, most churches are built with weekly gifts from a large number of small or average income families.

Before starting construction, make certain that you have funds in hand or loan commitments to take care of the contractor's payments as they become due and to assume responsibility for the architect's fee. Keeping your credit and a good name in the community is a very important part of your total building program.

Plan to keep your building debt, if it is at all possible, within 30 to 40 per cent of the total cost. Make certain that you have a plan of debt reduction which will insure all payments being met promptly. In this way you will relieve the church of serious embarrassment and maintain its good name in the community.

Plan to pay off the building debt in not more than ten years. After that period the building debt becomes an old story, interest on the debt runs very high proportionately, and it becomes exceedingly difficult to retire the unpaid portion of the indebtedness.

Have a special committee on memorial gifts, and give them the responsibility of controlling the nature of the memorials to be installed within the church edifice. Usually, this committee is required to submit proposed memorials to the official governing board of the church for their approval.

It is wise for the church to capitalize on all special days in the life of the church to procure extra gifts for the building fund. Even though you have put on a thorough "every member canvass," you will find that special appeals and memorial occasions in the life of the church will bring forth additional funds from those who have already pledged, the wealthier members of the church, those who have a sentimental attachment to the church building, and the newcomers who have joined the church since the initial campaign was inaugurated.

Be sure that you get the larger campaign objectives before your congregation rather than some of the secondary items which will tend to distract the enthusiasm and attention of the church as a whole from the major considerations.

As someone has well said: "You never can tell what people will give until you ask them."

Bibliography --

Adair, Thelma and McCort, Elizabeth. *How to Make Church School Equipment,* Westminster Press, 1955.

American School and University, Vols. 20 and 27, American School Publishing Company.

Andover Newton Theological School Bulletin, April, 1954. Betzner, Jean (compiler). *School Housing Needs of Young Children,* Association for Childhood Education. 1939.

Baird, Lulu Doyle. *The Church at Work with Primary Children.* Methodist Publishing House, 1953.

Blankenship, Lois. *Providing for the Children of the Church,* Judson Press.

Bowman, Clarice M. *Church-Agency Relationships,* National Council of Churches, 1954.

Briefs for Church Builders. A series of leaflets offering practical suggestions to churches that are considering building or remodeling.

Number 1   Church Parking
Number 2   Building on One Level—Or More
Number 3   The First Unit
Number 4   Musical Arrangements
Number 5   Light and Color
Number 6   Making a Church Homelike
Number 7   High Visibility for Your Church
Number 8   Sound Control
Number 9   Motivation for Building Churches
Number 10   Multiple Church and Church School
Number 11   A Proper Place for Everything
Number 12   A Home for the Minister
Number 13   Rooms for Pre-School Children
Number 14   Rooms for Primary and Junior Classes
Number 15   Rooms for Youth and Education Classes

Department of Audio-Visual and Broadcast Education, *Using Audio-Visuals in the Church,* National Council of Churches, 1950.

Department of Audio-Visual Instruction. *Planning Schools for Use of Audio-Visual Materials,* Booklets No. 1, 2, 3. National Education Association.

Domingos, Ann Maria. *Working with Children in the Small Church.* Methodist Publishing House. 1953.

Gable, Lee J. *Christian Nurture Through the Church,* National Council of Churches, 1955.

Gardner, Elizabeth C. *The 2's at Church,* Judson Press, 1953.

Haines, Marjorie. *When We Teach Primary Children,* Westminster Press, 1957.

Harrell, W. A. *Manual of Church Building Standards,* Department of Church Architecture, Southern Baptist Convention.

Harris, Jane B. *When We Teach Juniors,* Westminster Press, 1957.

Heaton, A. Beth. *The 3's at Church,* Judson Press, 1953.

Hefernan, Helen. *Space for Living* and *Stimulation for Learning.* Available National Education Assoc., 1201 16th Street, N.W., Washington 6, D. C.

Hoiland, Richard. A Compilation: *Planning Christian Education* in the Local Church. Judson Press.

Jones, Mary Alice. *Guiding Children in Christian Growth.* Abingdon-Cokesbury, 1949.

Illuminating Engineering Society. *School Lighting,* American Institute of Architects, 1948.

Illuminating Engineering Society. "Transactions of Illuminating Engineering Society," (London), Vol. 14, No. 5.

Klein, Sara. *When They Are Three,* Westminster Press, 1950.

White, Emma Jane Kramer. *Equipment and Arrangement for Children's Groups* in the Church, Board of Education, The Methodist Church. Revised edition.

McCarty, Margie. The Church Plans for Children. Methodist Publishing House, 1953.

Mowrey, Thelma. "Music for Children in the Church," *United Theological Bulletin* Vol. 54, No. 2, United Theological Seminary.

National Education Association Journal. "Together We Build." Reprint February, 1955.

Presbyterian Church U.S.A. (Unpublished manual) Church Building, New Church Building and Church Development. 1953 ff.

Randolph, H. S. and Maloney, Alice. A *Manual for Town and Country Churches,* Presbyterian Church in the U.S.A., 1950.

School Planning Laboratory. "Planning Tomorrow's Secondary Schools," Stanford University Press. 1954.

Tobey, Kathrene M. *When We Teach Kindergarten Children.* Westminster Press, 1957.

U.S. Department of Health, Education, and Welfare. *Designing Elementary Classrooms,* Special Publication No. 1.

Good and Bad School Plants. Special Publication No. 2.

Planning and Designing the Multipurpose Rooms in Elementary Schools, Special Publication No. 3.

Westinghouse Electric Corporation. *The A.B.C. for School Lighting.*

Wilson, Russell E. *Flexible Classrooms.* Carter Co., 51 W. Hancock Street, Detroit, Mich.

Index